Becker.

W9-BDJ-934

This textbook contains information that was current at the time of printing.
Your course software will be updated on a regular basis as the content
that is tested on the CPA Exam evolves and as we improve our materials.
Note the version reference below and select your replacement textbook
under Replacement Products at **becker.com/cpa-replacement-products**
to learn if a newer version of this book is available to be ordered.

CPA Exam Review

Auditing
Final Review

For Exams Scheduled
After December 31, 2020

V 3.5

COURSE DEVELOPMENT TEAM

Timothy F. Gearty, CPA, MBA, JD, CGMA . . . . Editor in Chief, Financial/Regulation (Tax) National Editor

Angeline S. Brown, CPA, CGMA. . . . . Sr. Director, Product Management

Valerie Funk Anderson, CPA . . . . Sr. Manager, Curriculum

Stephen Bergens, CPA . . . . Manager, Accounting Curriculum

Cheryl Costello, CPA, CGMA . . . . Sr. Specialist, Curriculum

Tom Cox, CPA, CMA . . . . Financial (GASB & NFP) National Editor

Steven J. Levin, JD . . . . Regulation (Law) National Editor

Danita De Jane . . . . Director, Course Development

Joe Antonio . . . . Manager, Course Development

Shelly McCubbins, MBA . . . . Project Manager, Course Development

CONTRIBUTING EDITORS

Teresa C. Anderson, CPA, CMA, MPA

Katie Barnette, CPA

Jim DeSimpelare, CPA, MBA

Tara Z. Fisher, CPA

Melisa F. Galasso, CPA

R. Thomas Godwin, CPA, CGMA

Holly Hawk, CPA, CGMA

Liliana Hickman-Riggs, CPA, CMA, CIA, CFE, CITP, CFF, CGMA, FCPA, MS

Patrice W. Johnson, CPA

Julie D. McGinty, CPA

Sandra McGuire, CPA, MBA

Stephanie Morris, CPA, MAcc

Michelle Moshe, CPA, DipIFR

Peter Olinto, JD, CPA

Sandra Owen, JD, MBA, CPA

Michelle M. Pace, CPA

Michael Potenza, CPA, JD

Jennifer J. Rivers, CPA

Josh Rosenberg, MBA, CPA, CFA, CFP

Jonathan R. Rubin, CPA, MBA

Michael Rybak, CPA, CFA

Denise M. Stefano, CPA, CGMA, MBA

Elizabeth Lester Walsh, CPA, CITP

Permissions

Material from *Uniform CPA Examination Selected Questions and Unofficial Answers*, 1989–2020, copyright © by American Institute of Certified Public Accountants, Inc., is reprinted and/or adapted with permission.

Any knowing solicitation or disclosure of any questions or answers included on any CPA Examination is prohibited.

Authoring

Final Review Sections

Auditing Section I | *Ethics, Professional Responsibilities, and General Principles* 15-25%

A   Terms of Engagement: Client Acceptance and Continuance

B   Terms of Engagement: Communication With the Predecessor Auditor

C   Terms of Engagement: Establishing an Understanding

D   Audit Documentation

E   Communication With Management and Those Charged With Governance

F   Communications Related to Internal Control

G   Ethics, Independence, and Professional Conduct

H   Quality Control

Auditing Section II | *Assessing Risk and Developing a Planned Response* 20-30%

A   Planning an Engagement

B   Understanding an Entity's Internal Control

C   Assessing Risks Due to Fraud

D   Risk Assessment Procedures

E   Assessing the Risk of Material Misstatement

F   Responding to Assessed Risk

G   Materiality

H   Planning for and Using the Work of Others

I   Specific Areas of Engagement Risk: Related Parties and Noncompliance

J   Specific Areas of Engagement Risk: Accounting Estimates and Fair Value

(continued on next page)

(continued)

Auditing Section III | *Performing Further Procedures and Obtaining Evidence* 30 -40 ?

A   Understanding Sufficient Appropriate Evidence

B   Sampling Techniques

C   Tests of Controls

D   Analytical Procedures

E   Substantive Procedures

F   Confirmations

G   Performing Specific Procedures to Obtain Evidence

H   Specific Matters That Require Special Consideration: Inventory and Investments

I   Specific Matters That Require Special Consideration: Attorney Letter

J   Specific Matters That Require Special Consideration: Going Concern

K   Internal Control Deficiencies

L   Written Representations

M   Subsequent Events

N   Subsequent Discovery of Facts

Auditing Section IV | *Forming Conclusions and Reporting* 15-25 %

A   Reports on Auditing Engagements

B   Integrated Audit Reports

C   Reports on Internal Controls

D   Reports on Attestation Engagements

E   Accounting and Review Service Engagements

F   Accounting and Review Service Engagement Reports

G   Other Information

H   Reports Required by Government Auditing Standards

I   Special Reports

Introduction

Final Review is a condensed review that reinforces your understanding of the most heavily tested concepts on the CPA Exam. It is designed to help focus your study time during those final days between your Becker CPA Exam Review course and your exam date.

This Book

Becker's Final Review is arranged based on the AICPA's blueprints. The blueprints outline the technical content to be tested on each of the four parts of the CPA Exam. The blueprints can be found in the back sections of Becker's main CPA textbooks.

The Software

The Final Review software uses an interactive eBook (IEB) format. Watch the introduction video in the Final Review software for a tour of the IEB features.

We recommend progressing through this course in the following order:

- Review the IEB content, including the video introduction to each topic and the lecture audio associated with each page of the IEB.
- Work the embedded multiple-choice questions for each topic as you progress through the content.
- Work the related multiple-choice questions in the question bank for each topic.
- Once you have completed all of the IEB sections, topics, and multiple-choice questions, do the practice Simulations in the software.

Becker Customer and Academic Support

You can access Becker's Customer and Academic Support from within the course software by clicking Contact Support at the top at:

cpa.becker.com

You can also access customer service and technical support by calling 1-877-CPA-EXAM (outside the U.S. +1-630-472-2213).

15-25/.

I

Ethics, Professional Responsibilities, and General Principles

You've got this.

This is the final stretch of your CPA Exam preparation – the Final Review. You've diligently studied these topics, and now it's crunch time. This Final Review has completely new content from the Becker CPA Exam Review and focuses on the key concepts on the CPA Exam. Remember, fortune favors the brave, but the CPA Exam favors the prepared.

Access Becker's Final Review

You can access Final Review under Additional Resources on each section home page when you log in to **cpa.becker.com** or when you use the mobile apps.

What's inside

Your Final Review is designed to mimic the actual CPA Exam, and has all-new task-based simulations with SkillMaster videos and all-new multiple-choice questions. If you need help at any point, remember that you still have access to the features of the CPA Exam Review, including:

- SkillMaster videos that coach you through task-based simulations in the four-part CPA course

- Access to 1-on-1 academic support from our experienced CPA instructors

- Unlimited practice tests to work on your weaknesses

You're not in it alone!

For tips, stories and advice, visit our blog at **becker.com/blog.** You can also collaborate with other Becker students studying AUD on our Facebook study group at **facebook.com/groups/BeckerAUDStudyGroup/.**

Exam day tips

We want you to be prepared and confident when exam day rolls around. Here are some tips to keep in mind:

+ Arrive at least 30 minutes early on exam day.

+ Bring your NTS and two forms of identification.

+ Your cell phone is NOT allowed in the testing center, even during scheduled breaks.

+ No outside calculators are allowed. The testing software will have a built-in calculator for you to use.

+ Breathe. Relax. Ground yourself. You've got this.

Becker

Join the community!

1 Client Acceptance and Continuance Policies

The auditor should consider the firm's client acceptance and continuance policies, including:

- The firm's ability to meet reporting deadlines.
- The firm's ability to staff the engagement.
- Independence.
- Integrity of client management.

2 Preconditions for an Audit

Before accepting an audit engagement, the auditor should establish that the preconditions for an audit are present.

2.1 Financial Reporting Framework

The auditor should determine whether the financial reporting framework used by the client is acceptable.

2.2 Management Responsibilities

The auditor should obtain the agreement of management that it acknowledges and understands its responsibility:

- For the preparation and fair presentation of the financial statements
- For the design, implementation, and maintenance of internal control
- To provide the auditor with:
  - access to all information of which management is aware that is relevant to the preparation and fair presentation of the financial statements;
  - additional information that the auditor may request from management for the purpose of the audit; and
  - unrestricted access to persons within the entity from whom the auditor determines it is necessary to obtain audit evidence.

Question 1 | MCQ-09795

Which of the following auditor concerns most likely would be so serious that the auditor would conclude that a financial statement audit *cannot* be performed?

1. The CPA lacks experience in the client's operations and industry.

2. A portion of supporting evidence stored at an offsite storage facility was destroyed by a hurricane.

3. Management has imposed a restriction that the auditor believes will result in a qualified opinion.

4. There is substantial risk of management intentionally manipulating accounting records.

1 Communication Before Engagement Acceptance

Contact with the predecessor auditor before engagement acceptance is mandatory, but client permission is required. Inquiries can be oral or written. Inquiries should be made regarding:

- management integrity.
- disagreements with the predecessor auditor (principles, procedures, etc).
- reason for the change in auditors.
- any fraud, noncompliance with laws and regulations, or internal control matters and their communication to management, the audit committee, and those charged with governance.
- fee payment problems.

2 Communication During the Audit

- The auditor should obtain sufficient appropriate audit evidence about whether:
  - opening balances contain misstatements that could materially affect the current period financial statements; and
  - accounting policies reflected in the opening balances have been consistently applied.

- In order to do this, the auditor should request that management authorize the predecessor auditor to allow a review of the predecessor's audit documentation related to the most recently completed audit. The predecessor ordinarily allows a review of:
  - Planning documentation
  - Risk assessment procedures
  - Further audit procedures
  - Audit results
  - Matters of continuing accounting and audit significance

Question 1 MCQ-09796

A successor auditor's inquiries of the predecessor auditor should include questions regarding:

1. The number of engagement personnel the predecessor assigned to the engagement.

2. The assessment of the objectivity of the client's internal audit function.

3. Communications to management and those charged with governance regarding significant deficiencies in internal control.

4. The response rate for confirmations of accounts receivable.

1 Agree to the Terms of the Engagement

Establishing an agreement with the client is required to reduce the risk of misinterpretation. The agreement with the client should be documented through a written engagement letter. The agreement should include:

- The objective of the audit
- Management's responsibilities
- The auditor's responsibilities
- Limitations of the engagement
- Identification of the applicable financial reporting framework
- Reference to the expected form and content of any reports to be issued

On recurring audits, the auditor should assess whether circumstances require the terms of the engagement to be revised.

Question 1
MCQ-09799

An auditor's engagement letter most likely would include a statement regarding:

1. The advantages of statistical sampling.
2. The inherent limitations of an audit.
3. Billings to be paid in the form of stock of the entity.
4. The assessment of risk of material misstatement.

---

1 Audit Documentation (Working Papers)

Audit documentation is a written record of the work performed, evidence obtained, and conclusions reached. Audit documentation:

- is divided into permanent and current files.
- supports the auditor's report/opinion.
- aids in training and in the conduct/supervision of the audit.
- provides a record of accumulated evidence.
- must indicate that the accounting records reconcile with the financial statement.
- must contain enough information to allow an experienced auditor with no previous connection to the audit to understand the work that was performed.

2 Assembly and Retention

Audit documentation is required to be:

- assembled within 45 days (public company audits) or 60 days (other audits) following the report release date.
- kept for seven years (public company audits) or five years (other audits).

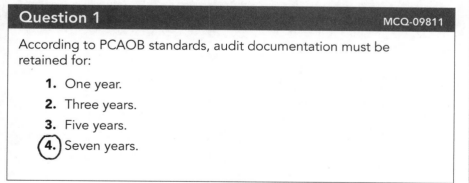

Question 1   MCQ-09811

According to PCAOB standards, audit documentation must be retained for:

1. One year.
2. Three years.
3. Five years.
4. Seven years.

3 Ownership and Confidentiality

Audit documentation is the independent auditor's property. It is confidential, but can be disclosed without client permission as part of:

- a quality review program.
- the subpoena process.
- an investigation conducted by the AICPA, state CPA society, or under state statute.

Question 2   MCQ-09844

According to professional standards, audit documentation should:

1. Be prepared in enough detail so that a new staff auditor who has no previous connection with the audit can understand the conclusions reached and any significant judgments made to reach those conclusions.

2. Monitor the effectiveness of the CPA firm's quality control activities.

3. Show who performed the work and the date the work was completed.

4. Include a flowchart to show the design and implementation of internal control.

---

4 Tickmarks

Auditors often use tickmarks, or symbols indicating the work that has been performed.

American Manufacturers Inc.
LONG-TERM DEBT
October 31, 20X7

Lender	Interest Rate	Payment Terms	Collateral	Balance 10/31/X6	Current Year Borrowings	Current Year Reductions	Balance 10/31/X7	Interest Paid To	Accrued Interest Payable 10/31/X7	Comments
▲ First National Bank	10%	Interest only on last day of each quarter; principal due in full on 9/30/X9.	Manufacturing equipment	500,000 ■	200,000 ◆ 3/31/X7	(100,000) O 6/30/X7	600,000 ✓	9/30/X7	5,000 �':'	First National confirms that interest payments are current and agrees with account balance.
▲ Second State Bank	9%	$10,000 principal plus interest due on the 1st of each month; due in full on 1/1/X0.	First mortgage on production facilities	380,000 ■	0	(110,000) +	270,000 ✓★	9/30/X7	2,025 ▼	Monthly payment for $12,025 was mailed on 11/3/X7; Second State agrees with account balance.
▲ Third Savings & Loan	12%	$5,000 principal plus interest due on the 15th of each month; due in full on 10/15/X9.	Second mortgage on production facilities	180,000 ■	0	(60,000)	120,000 ✱★	10/15/X7	600	Third Savings & Loan claims 10/15/X7 payment wasn't received as of 11/5/X7; adjusting entry proposed to increase balance $5,000 and increase accrued interest payable.
▲ A. Clark, majority stockholder	0%	Due in full 10/31/X9.	Unsecured	700,000 ■	0	(200,000) 10/28/X7	500,000 ✓		0	Borrowed additional $200,000 from Clark on 11/5/X7; need to investigate reborrowing just after year-end and consider imputed interest on 0% stockholder loan.
				1,760,000	200,000	(470,000)	1,490,000 ●		7,625 ●	

Tickmark Legend

▲ Agreed interest rate, terms, and collateral to note & loan agreement.	✓ Confirmed, without exception.
■ Traced amount to prior year's audit documentation	★ Reclassification entry proposed for current portion of long-term debt.
◆ Agreed to loan agreement, validated bank deposit ticket, and board of director's authorization.	✱ Confirmed, with exception.
O Agreed to canceled check and board of director's authorization.	● Traced amount to current year's trial balance and general ledger.
+ Agreed to canceled checks and lender's monthly statements.	▼ Tested reasonableness of calculations.

1 Those Charged With Governance

Those charged with governance are those who bear responsibility to oversee the obligations and strategic direction of an entity, including the board of directors and the audit committee.

1.1 Audit Committee

An audit committee is a subgroup of those charged with governance. An audit committee consists of members of the board of directors, usually three to five "outside" directors, who are neither employees nor part of management and who do not have a material financial interest in the company. Audit committees are meant to strengthen the public's sense of the independence of the public accountant. Audit committee functions include:

- establishing the control environment.
- selecting and appointing the independent auditor.
- reviewing of the quality of the auditor's work.
- reviewing of the scope of the audit.
- responding to any auditor recommendations.
- helping to resolve disagreements related to the accounting treatment of material items.
- providing a bridge between the board of directors and the auditor.

2 Required Communications

The following items should be communicated to those charged with governance:

2.1 Matters Related to the Auditor's Responsibility

- The auditor is responsible for expressing an opinion on the financial statement, following GAAS, and communicating significant matters related to the financial statement audit.
- Internal control is considered as part of planning the audit, not as a means of expressing an opinion on the effectiveness of internal control (nonissuers).
- An audit does not relieve management or those charged with governance of their responsibilities.

2.2 An Overview of the Planned Scope and Timing of the Audit

■ The auditor may communicate how significant risks of material misstatement will be addressed, the planned approach toward internal control, factors affecting materiality, and any potential use of internal audit staff.

■ The auditor may also solicit information from those charged with governance, such as the entity's objectives, strategies, and risks, or matters to which the auditor should pay particular attention.

■ The communication may also include discussion of the attitudes, awareness, and actions of those charged with governance.

2.3 Significant Audit Findings

■ The auditor should communicate:

- The auditor's views about qualitative aspects of the entity's accounting practices.

- Significant difficulties encountered in performing the audit, or disagreements with management, whether or not resolved.

- Uncorrected, nontrivial misstatements.

- Other issues that the auditor judges to be significant.

■ If those charged with governance are not involved with managing the entity, the auditor should also communicate material, corrected misstatements resulting from the audit, management representations requested by the auditor, management's consultation with other accountants, and significant issues arising from the audit that were discussed with management.

■ The auditor may also request additional information from those charged with governance.

2.4 Additional Requirements for Issuers

Auditors of issuers are required to report to the audit committee all critical accounting policies, all material alternative GAAP accounting treatments, and other material communications between the auditor and management (e.g., management letters, schedules of unadjusted differences, etc.). In addition, auditors of issuers should discuss and provide a draft of the auditor's report to the audit committee. If no formal audit committee exists, communications should be made to the full board of directors.

Question 1

Which of the following statements is correct about an auditor's required communication with those charged with governance?

1. Any matters communicated to those charged with governance also are required to be communicated to the entity's management.

2. The auditor is required to inform those charged with governance about significant misstatements discovered by the auditor and subsequently corrected by management.

3. Disagreements with management about the application of accounting principles must be communicated in writing to those charged with governance.

4. The auditor should not communicate frequently recurring misstatements unless they are material.

3 Form and Timing of Communication

In general, communications may be oral or in writing. Significant audit findings should be communicated in writing when, in the auditor's judgment, oral communication would be inadequate.

■ Written communications should include a limitation on the use of the communication.

■ Oral communications should be documented; copies of written communications should be retained.

■ For nonissuers, timing of the communications should occur in a manner that allows appropriate action to be taken.

■ For issuers, communications should be made before the issuance of the auditor's report.

Auditing Final Review

Question 2   MCQ-09055

Which of the following items are included in the auditor's communication to those charged with governance and in management's representation letter to the auditor?

I. The auditor's responsibility under generally accepted auditing standards.

II. Management's responsibility for fair presentation of the financial statements in conformity with generally accepted accounting principles.

III. Uncorrected, nontrivial misstatements identified by the auditor.

	Auditor's Communication to Those Charged with Governance	Management Representation Letter
1.	I and III, only	II and III, only
2.	I, II, and III	I and II, only
3.	I and II, only	I, II, and III
4.	I, only	II, only

1 Responsibility of the Auditor in a Financial Statement Audit Only

The auditor is not required to search for deficiencies that are less severe than a material weakness, or to express an opinion on internal control The auditor may, however, become aware of control deficiencies while performing the audit.

- Both significant deficiencies and material weaknesses must be communicated, in writing, to management and those charged with governance within 60 days of the report release date.

- Previously communicated significant deficiencies and material weaknesses that have not been corrected should be communicated again, in writing, during the current audit.

- The auditor should communicate to management only, in writing or orally, other deficiencies identified during the audit that are of sufficient importance to merit management's attention but that are not significant deficiencies or material weaknesses.

- The auditor may not report the absence of significant deficiencies, but may report on the absence of material weaknesses.

Question 1

MCQ-09061

Jefferson, CPA, has identified five significant deficiencies in internal control during the audit of Portico Industries, a nonissuer. Two of these conditions are considered to be material weaknesses. Which best describes Jefferson's communication requirements?

1. Communicate the two material weaknesses to Portico's management and those charged with governance, but not the three significant deficiencies that are not material weaknesses.

2. Communicate all five significant deficiencies to Portico's management and those charged with governance, distinguishing between significant deficiencies and material weaknesses.

3. Communicate all five significant deficiencies to Portico's management and those charged with governance, but only require a management response with respect to the two material weaknesses.

4. Communicate all five significant deficiencies to Portico's management and those charged with governance, without distinction among the deficiencies.

2 Internal Control Communication (Nonissuers)

Independent Auditor's Report

To Management and [*identify the body or individuals charged with governance*] of ABC Company:

In planning and performing our audit of the financial statements of ABC Company (the "Company") as of and for the year ended December 31, 20XX, in accordance with auditing standards generally accepted in the United States of America, we considered the Company's internal control over financial reporting (internal control) as a basis for designing audit procedures that are appropriate in the circumstances for the purpose of expressing our opinion on the financial statements, but not for the purpose of expressing an opinion on the effectiveness of the Company's internal control. Accordingly, we do not express an opinion on the effectiveness of the Company's internal control.

Our consideration of internal control was for the limited purpose described in the preceding paragraph and was not designed to identify all deficiencies in internal control that might be material weaknesses or significant deficiencies and therefore, material weaknesses or significant deficiencies may exist that were not identified. However, as discussed below, we identified certain deficiencies in internal control that we consider to be material weaknesses and significant deficiencies.

A deficiency in internal control exists when the design or operation of a control does not allow management or employees, in the normal course of performing their assigned functions, to prevent, or detect and correct, misstatements on a timely basis. A material weakness is a deficiency, or a combination of deficiencies, in internal control, such that there is a reasonable possibility that a material misstatement of the entity's financial statements will not be prevented, or detected and corrected on a timely basis. We consider the following deficiencies in the Company's internal control to be material weaknesses:

[*Describe the material weaknesses that were identified and an explanation of their potential effects.*]

A significant deficiency is a deficiency, or combination of deficiencies, in internal control that is less severe than a material weakness, yet important enough to merit attention by those charged with governance. We consider the following deficiencies in the Company's internal control to be significant deficiencies:

[*Describe the significant deficiencies that were identified and an explanation of their potential effects.*]

[*If the auditor is communicating significant deficiencies and did not identify any material weaknesses, the auditor may state that none of the identified deficiencies are considered to be material weaknesses.*]

This communication is intended solely for the information and use of management, [*identify the body or individuals charged with governance*], others within the organization, and [*identify any specified governmental authorities to which the auditor is required to report*] and is not intended to be, and should not be, used by anyone other than these specified parties.

[*Auditor's Signature*]
[*Date*]

1 AICPA Code of Professional Conduct

1.1 Independence Rule

1.1.1 Independence Requirement

- Independence is required for audits and attest services.
- It is not required for compilations, consulting services or tax work.

1.1.2 Independence Is Impaired in the Following Cases

- Independence is impaired if the CPA has a direct financial interest, regardless of materiality or a material indirect interest.
- Independence is impaired if audit fees remain unpaid for more than one year prior to the issuance of the current audit report. It is considered a loan.
- Independence is impaired if a CPA has a management position with a client or is an employee. The spouse of a CPA can be an employee, but cannot hold a management position.
- Independence is impaired if a CPA makes hiring decisions for a client. The CPA may recommend a job description, screen candidates for the position, and advise the client on hiring.
- Litigation can impair independence, but not for immaterial dollar amounts unrelated to the audit.

1.1.3 Independence Is Not Impaired in the Following Cases

- Independence is not impaired with a bank client by a checking account that is fully insured.
- Independence is not impaired by a fully collateralized auto loan.

1.2 Integrity and Objectivity Rule

- All engagements must be performed with objectivity and integrity.
- The CPA should be free of conflict of interests, although services may still be performed if a conflict is disclosed to the client and the client consents to the CPA performing the engagement.

1.3 General Standards Rule

The general standards apply to all engagements.

1.3.1 Professional Competence

Requires proper education and training. The CPA need not be an expert or attain specialty accreditation. The CPA can consult with or hire experts.

1.3.2 Due Professional Care

The CPA must exercise the same skill a reasonably prudent accountant would. The CPA must critically review the work done by others.

1.3.3 Adequate Planning and Supervision

All engagements must be adequately planned and supervised.

1.3.4 Sufficient Relevant Data

All decisions must be based on sufficient relevant data.

1.4 Compliance With Standards Rule and Accounting Principles Rule

- A CPA performing an engagement must comply with applicable standards.

- A CPA cannot state that financial statements or other data comply with GAAP if there are departures that would have a material effect on the financial statements.

- Unusual circumstances may justify a departure from GAAP if compliance would cause the financial statements to be misleading (e.g., new legislation or new form of business practice). The departure from GAAP must be described and explained.

1.5 Confidential Client Information Rule

Confidential client information cannot be revealed to others without the client's consent. Confidential information can be revealed in a lawsuit and it can be revealed to a state CPA society voluntary quality control review panel. It also can be revealed when subpoenaed and confidential audit documentation can be reviewed by a prospective purchaser of a CPA's practice if confidentiality is assured (but audit documentation may not be turned over to a purchaser without the client's consent).

1.6 Contingent Fees Rule

A contingent fee is a fee dependent upon attaining a specified result. It is not permitted for audits, reviews and most tax work. Contingent fees are permitted for compilations if the CPA discloses the lack of independence. It is also permitted if a CPA represents a client in an examination of a tax return by the IRS.

1.7 Acts Discreditable Rule

The following acts are considered discreditable to the profession:

- Retaining a client's records after the client has demanded that the records be returned or after the employment relationship has been terminated.

- Discrimination in employment.

- Failure to follow standards in audits or government audits.

- Negligently making false or misleading journal entries.

- Failure to timely file tax returns or remit payroll taxes.
- Soliciting or disclosing CPA exam questions or answers.
- Makes false, misleading, or deceptive claims about the member's abilities to provide professional services.
- Disclosure of confidential information, obtained from a prospective client or non-client without consent.

Question 1   MCQ-09616

Smith and Company, CPAs, has been hired to perform the audit of Warehouse Company's Year 10 financial statements. Warehouse Company is an issuer. Under the ethical standards of the profession, which of the following employment relationships would not impair Smith and Company's independence?

1. The lead partner on the audit serves on Warehouse Company's board of directors.

2. The Warehouse Company's former controller, who left the company during Year 10, is assigned to the engagement team that will perform the Warehouse Company audit.

3. The wife of an audit engagement team member works in Warehouse Company's customer service department.

4. The former manager of the Warehouse engagement was hired as Warehouse Company's CFO during Year 10.

Question 2   MCQ-09477

The concept of materiality would be *least* important to an auditor when considering the:

1. Adequacy of disclosure of a client's illegal act.

2. Discovery of weaknesses in a client's internal control structure.

3. Effects of a direct financial interest in the client on the CPA's independence.

4. Decision whether to use positive or negative confirmations of accounts receivable.

2 AICPA Conceptual Framework Approach

The rules and interpretations of the AICPA Code of Professional Conduct (discussed above) seek to address many situations; however, they cannot address all relationships or circumstances that may arise. In the absence of an interpretation that addresses a particular relationship or circumstance, a member should apply the appropriate conceptual framework approach.

The conceptual framework approach requires entities to identify threats to compliance with the fundamental principles, evaluate the significance of the threat, and apply safeguards to eliminate threats or reduce threats to an acceptable level, whenever possible.

2.1 Threats to Compliance

Threats to compliance may fall into one or more of the following categories:

2.1.1 Adverse Interest Threat

The threat that a member will not act with objectivity because the member's interests are opposed to the interests of the client or employing organization.

2.1.2 Advocacy Threat

The threat that a member will promote the interests of the client or employing organization to the point that his or her objectivity or independence, as applicable, is compromised.

2.1.3 Familiarity Threat

The threat that, due to a long or close relationship with the client or employing organization, a member will become too accepting of the product or service and/or too sympathetic to the client's or employing organization's interests.

2.1.4 Management Participation Threat

The threat that a member will take on the role of client management or otherwise assume management responsibilities. This threat exits for members engaged in attest engagements.

2.1.5 Self-Interest Threat

The threat that a member could benefit financially or otherwise from an interest in, or relationship with, a client or employing organization, or persons associated with the client or employing organization.

2.1.6 Self-Review Threat

The threat that a member will not appropriately evaluate the results of a previous judgment made, or service performed or supervised, by the member or an individual in the member's firm or employing organization, and that the member will rely on that service in forming a judgment as part of another service.

2.1.7 Undue Influence Threat

The threat that a member will subordinate his or her judgment to an individual associated with a client or employing organization or any relevant third party due to that individual's reputation or expertise, aggressive or dominant personality, or attempts to coerce or exercise excessive influence over the member.

2.2 Safeguards

Safeguards may include those created by the profession, legislation, or regulation, implemented by the client or employing organization, and/or implemented by the firm (if applicable).

3 Sarbanes-Oxley Act of 2002

The Sarbanes-Oxley Act of 2002 created the Public Company Accounting Oversight Board (PCAOB) and outlined the following key standards and independence rules that apply to audits of issuers:

3.1 Records Retention

Audit workpapers and supporting documentation must be maintained for seven years.

3.2 Concurring Partner Review

A concurring or second partner review is required for each audit report.

3.3 Prohibited Services

A registered public accounting firm may not provide the following services for issuers:

- Bookkeeping
- Financial information systems design and implementation
- Appraisal and valuation services
- Actuarial services
- Management functions or human resources services
- Internal audit outsourcing services
- Services as a broker, dealer, investment advisor, or investment banker
- Legal services
- Expert services unrelated to the audit

Tax services may be performed if preapproved by the audit committee.

3.4   Audit Committee Preapproval and Reporting

All audit services and permitted non-audit services must be preapproved by the audit committee. Additionally, the auditor must report the following to the audit committees of audited corporations:

- Critical accounting policies and practices used
- Alternative accounting treatments discussed with management and the treatment preferred by the auditors
- Material written communications between the auditor and management

3.5   Audit Partner Rotation

The lead and reviewing partner must rotate off the audit every five years.

3.6   Conflicts of Interest

The audit firm cannot have employed the issuer's CEO, CFO, controller, or chief accounting officer, or equivalent, for a one-year period preceding the audit (the "cooling off" period).

Question 3   MCQ-09589

Which of the following is not a provision of the Sarbanes-Oxley Act of 2002?

1. The auditor of an issuer may not provide internal audit outsourcing services for the issuer.
2. Audit documentation must be maintained for five years.
3. The lead and reviewing partners must rotate off the audit after five years.
4. Tax services must be preapproved by the audit committee.

---

4 Public Company Accounting Oversight Board (PCAOB)

4.1   Interim Standards

The PCAOB has adopted the Independence Rule and Integrity and Objectivity Rule from the AICPA Code of Professional Conduct on an interim basis.

4.2   Independence Standards

The PCAOB enforces the provisions of SOX described above and has issued the following additional independence standards that apply to audits of issuers by registered firms:

4.2.1   Contingent Fees

A registered firm may not provide services or products for a contingent fee or commission.

4.2.2   Tax Services

A registered firm may not provide to audit clients any tax services related to certain confidential or aggressive tax transactions and may not provide tax services to corporate officers of audit clients, or the immediate family members of corporate officers.

Proposed tax services and related fees must be communicated to the audit committee in writing and the potential effects of the tax services on audit independence must be discussed with the audit committee and documented.

4.2.3   Non-audit Services Related to Internal Control Over Financial Reporting

Non-audit services related to internal control over financial reporting must be communicated to the audit committee in writing and the potential effects of the tax services on audit independence must be discussed with the audit committee and documented.

4.2.4   Communication With the Audit Committee Concerning Independence

Before accepting an initial engagement with an issuer, and at least annually for each issuer audit client, a registered firm must describe in writing to the audit committee all relationships that might affect independence and the effects of those relationships. As part of the annual communication, the firm must affirm its independence in writing as of the date of the communication.

5 U.S. Securities and Exchange Commission (SEC)

Rule 2-01 of SEC Regulation S-X outlines the independence rules that apply to the auditors of SEC registrants. The SOX independence rules have been incorporated into these rules. According to Regulation S-X, the following circumstances impair auditor independence:

5.1 Financial Relationships

Similar to the AICPA Code of Professional Conduct, the SEC prohibits any direct or material indirect financial interest in an audit client, as well as loans to or from an audit client (other than loans from financial institutions under normal lending circumstances). Additionally, the audit client may not invest in the accounting firm or engage the accounting firm to provide investments services.

5.2 Employment Relationships

Independence is impaired by employment relationships between the accounting firm, covered members of the accounting firm, and the audit client, including:

- Employment of a covered person by the audit client or service on the audit client board of directors.
- Employment of a close family member of a covered person in an accounting or financial reporting role at an audit client.
- Employment at the audit client of a former member of the audit engagement team in an accounting or financial oversight role, unless the individual no longer influences the accounting firms operations, and has no capital balances or financial arrangements with the accounting firm.
- Employment at the audit client of a former member of the audit engagement team in a financial oversight role during the one-year preceding the commencement of audit procedures.
- Employment at the accounting firm of former employees of the audit client, unless the individual does not participate in or influence any audit related to the period in which the individual was employed by the client.

5.3 Performance of Non-audit Services

The prohibited non-audit services outlined under SOX (see above) are also prohibited by the SEC.

5.4 Contingent Fees

Independence is impaired by contingent fee or commission arrangements between the auditor and the audit client.

5.5   Failure to Rotate Partners

The SEC has enhanced the SOX partner rotation rules. The SEC requires the lead and concurring partner to rotate off the audit engagement after five years and requires other audit partners to rotate off the audit engagement after seven years. Lead and concurring partners are subject to a five-year time out period before returning to an engagement and other audit partners are subject to a two-year time out period.

5.6   Failure of the Audit Committee to Administer the Engagement

The audit committee must preapprove all audit, review, and attestation engagements and all permissible non-audit services. Consistent with SOX, the auditor must report the following to the audit committees of audited corporations:

- Critical accounting policies and practices used.
- Alternative accounting treatments discussed with management and the treatment preferred by the auditors.
- Material written communications between the auditor and management.

5.7   Certain Compensation Arrangements

An audit partner cannot earn or receive compensation based on selling engagements to audit clients for services other than audit, review or attest services.

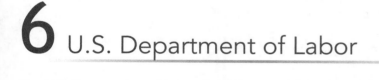

6   U.S. Department of Labor

The U.S. Department of Labor (DOL) has established guidelines for determining when a qualified public accountant is independent for the purpose of rendering an opinion on an employee benefit plan under the Employee Retirement Income Security Act of 1974 (ERISA).

6.1   Independence Required

Auditor independence is required when auditing and rendering an opinion on the financial information required to be submitted to the Employee Benefits Security Administration of the DOL.

6.2 Impairment of Independence

The following situations impair independence with respect to an employee benefit plan:

- Any direct financial interest or a material indirect financial interest in the plan or the plan sponsor.

- Connection to the plan or the plan sponsor as a promoter, underwriter, investment advisor, voting trustee, director, officer, or employee.

- An accountant or a member of the accounting firm maintains financial records for the employee benefit plan.

6.3 Independence Not Impaired

An accountant's independence is not impaired when:

- A former officer or employee of the plan or plan sponsor is employed by the firm, the individual has completely disassociated for the plan or plan sponsor, and the individual does not participate in auditing the financial statements of the plan covering any period of his or her employment by the plan or plan sponsor.

- The accountant or the accountant's firm was engaged by the plan sponsor during the period of the professional engagement with the employee benefit plan.

- An actuary associated with the accountant or the accountant's firm rendered services to the plan.

Question 4   MCQ-09603

Which of the following will not impair independence under the U.S. Department of Labor's independence rules for audits of employee benefit plans?

1. An actuary employed by the audit firm performs services for the employee benefit plan.

2. The audit firm has a material indirect financial interest in the sponsor of the employee benefit plan.

3. A member of the audit firm maintains the financial records of the employee benefit plan.

4. A partner on the engagement team serves on the board of directors of the plan sponsor.

---

7 GAGAS Conceptual Framework for Independence

7.1 Requirements

The GAGAS independence conceptual framework steps require that an auditor:

- Identify threats to independence;
- Evaluate the significance of the threats identified, both individually and in the aggregate; and
- Apply safeguards as necessary to eliminate the threats or reduce them to an acceptable level.

If no safeguards are available to eliminate an unacceptable threat or reduce it to an acceptable level, independence would be considered to be impaired.

7.2 Threats to Independence

- Self-interest threat is the threat that a financial or other interest will inappropriately influence an auditor's judgment or behavior.
- Self-review threat is the threat that an auditor providing non-audit services will not appropriately evaluate the results of previous judgments made or services when significant to an audit.
- Bias threat is the threat that the auditor's position is not objective.
- Familiarity threat is the threat that aspects of a relationship, such as a close or long relationship, will lead an auditor to take a position that is not objective.
- Undue influence threat is the threat that external influences or pressures will impact an auditor's ability to make independent and objective judgments.
- Management participation threat is the threat that results from an auditor's taking on the role of management or otherwise performing management functions on behalf of the entity undergoing an audit.
- Structural threat is the threat that occurs when an audit organization's placement within a government entity might impact the audit organization's ability to perform work and report results objectively.

7.3 Safeguards

- Safeguards are controls designed to eliminate or reduce to an acceptable level threats to independence.
- Under the conceptual framework, the auditor applies safeguards that address the specific facts and circumstances under which threats to independence exist.

7.4 Evaluation of Non-audit Services

- The auditor should determine whether providing a non-audit service would create a threat to independence.
- A critical component of this determination is consideration of management's ability to effectively oversee the non-audit service to be performed.

Auditing Final Review

1 Quality Control Standards

1.1 System of Quality Control

CPA firms are required to adopt a system of quality control for their auditing, attestation, and accounting and review services.

1.1.1 Human Resources

A firm should have criteria for recruitment and hiring, determining capabilities and competencies, assigning personnel to engagements, professional development, and performance evaluation, compensation and advancement.

1.1.2 Engagement/Client Acceptance and Continuance

Policies and procedures should ensure that the firm minimizes the likelihood of association with a client whose management lacks integrity, undertakes only those engagements that the firm expects to complete with reasonable competence, and complies with legal and ethical requirements.

1.1.3 Leadership Responsibilities

The firm's leadership bears the ultimate responsibility for the firm's quality control system and should create a culture that emphasizes quality.

1.1.4 Engagement Performance

Policies and procedures should be established to ensure that the firm consistently achieves a high level of performance, that engagements are properly supervised, that confidentiality, safe custody, integrity, accessibility, retrievability, and retention of engagement documentation is maintained, that differences of opinion can be resolved, and that guidelines exist to determine when an engagement quality control review should be performed.

1.1.5 Monitoring

The firm should have reasonable assurance that its quality control system is relevant, adequate, operating effectively, and complied with in practice.

1.1.6 Ethical Requirements

Personnel should maintain independence in fact and appearance in all required circumstances, perform all professional responsibilities with integrity, and maintain objectivity in discharging professional responsibilities.

1.2 Deficiencies or Noncompliance

Deficiencies in, or noncompliance with, a firm's quality control standards do not necessarily imply that a specific engagement was not performed in accordance with appropriate standards.

Question 1

A CPA firm should adopt a system of quality control:

1. For all audit and attest services, but not necessarily for accounting and review services.

2. That encompasses human resource policies and practices.

3. Because it maximizes audit efficiency.

4. Because it ensures that all audit engagements will be conducted in accordance with generally accepted auditing standards.

II

Assessing Risk and Developing a Planned Response

1 Obtain Knowledge of Industry and Business

The auditor is not required to have prior experience with the client's business or industry before accepting the engagement, but must obtain an understanding of the business and industry once the engagement has been accepted.

1.1 Industry Knowledge

Industry knowledge can be obtained from:

- AICPA accounting and auditing guides
- Trade publications and professional trade associations
- Government publications
- GAAP Financial Statements - Best Practices in Presentation and Disclosure

1.2 Business Knowledge

Knowledge of the client's business can be obtained by:

- Touring client facilities
- Reviewing the client's financial history
- Obtaining an understanding of the client's accounting system
- Asking questions of client personnel

Question 1   MCQ-09804

Which of the following procedures would a CPA *least likely* perform during the planning stage of the audit?

1. Determine the timing of testing.
2. Take a tour of the client's facilities.
3. Perform inquiries of outside legal counsel regarding pending litigation.
4. Determine the effect of information technology on the audit.

---

2 Audit Strategy and Audit Plan

2.1 Audit Strategy

The auditor should establish an overall audit strategy, including preliminary assessments of materiality. The audit strategy outlines the scope of the audit engagement, the reporting objectives, timing of the audit, required communications, and the factors that determine the focus of the audit.

2.2 Audit Plan

The auditor is required to develop a written audit plan that outlines the nature, extent, and timing of the procedures to be performed during the audit, including:

- Risk assessment procedures
- Further audit procedures (tests of controls and substantive procedures)
- Other audit procedures

The audit strategy and audit plan can be modified as the audit progresses in response to new information or to the results of other procedures.

Question 2   MCQ-09072

Which of the following is required documentation in an audit in accordance with generally accepted auditing standards?

1. A flowchart or narrative of the information system relevant to financial reporting describing the recording and classification of transactions for financial reporting.

2. An audit plan setting forth in detail the procedures necessary to accomplish the engagement's objectives.

3. A planning memorandum establishing the timing of the audit procedures and coordinating the assistance of entity personnel.

4. An internal control questionnaire identifying controls that assure specific objectives will be achieved.

---

1 Overview of Internal Control

1.1 Definition

Internal control is a process designed to provide assurance that an entity's objectives will be achieved. Objectives include:

- Reliability of financial reporting
- Effectiveness and efficiency of operations
- Compliance with applicable laws and regulations

1.2 Inherent Limitations

- Human error
- Collusion, deliberate circumvention, fraud
- Management override

Question 1   MCQ-09071

Which of the following situations is *not* an example of an inherent limitation of internal control?

1. A programming error in the design of an automated control allows an employee to give himself an unauthorized pay increase.

2. A lack of physical controls over the safeguarding of assets allows an employee to steal company assets.

3. Management's failure to enforce control policies surrounding access to inventory allows employees to steal assets.

4. A fraud scheme whereby an employee orders personal goods and his supervisor, who is in on the scheme, signs the checks to pay for those goods.

---

2 Five Components of Internal Control

> Mnemonic = **CRIME**

2.1 Control Environment

Sets the tone of an organization and its policies and procedures.
Key points include:

- Integrity
- Competence
- Participation of those charged with governance
- Management philosophy
- Organizational structure
- Role assignment
- Promotion and training

2.2 Risk Assessment

Management identifies, analyzes, and manages risks that affect the
entity's ability to accomplish its major objectives. Once risks are identified,
management considers their significance, likelihood of occurrence, and
how they should be managed. Key points include:

- New products
- Rapid growth
- Other changes

2.3 Information and Communication Systems

Methods and records used to identify, capture, and exchange information.
Key points include:

- All transactions are recorded and complete
- Detailed enough to provide for adequate financial reporting disclosure
- Communication among management, employees, those charged with
  governance, and external parties

2.4 Monitoring

Procedures established to assess the quality of the internal control
structure, and to make necessary corrections. Key points include:

- Internal audit
- Review and independent checks
- Other procedures such as mailing customer statements

2.5   (Existing) Control Activities

Policies and procedures established to ensure that management objectives are carried out. Key points include:

> Mnemonic = **PAID TIPS**

- **P**renumbering of documents
- **A**uthorization of transactions
- **I**ndependent checks to maintain asset accountability
- **D**ocumentation
- **T**imely and appropriate performance reviews
- **I**nformation processing controls
- **P**hysical controls for safeguarding assets
- **S**egregation of duties

3 Audit Requirements

The auditor should:

- understand the five components of internal control.
- evaluate the design of relevant controls and determine whether they have been implemented.
- assess risk.
- design appropriate audit procedures, based on assessed risk.

Question 2   MCQ-09054

Which of the following is true regarding performance of the following audit tasks while obtaining an understanding of internal control?

Audit Tasks:

I.   Obtain an understanding of the design of controls.

II. Determine whether internal controls have been implemented.

III. Evaluate the operating effectiveness of controls.

1. The auditor must perform I and II, and is allowed, but not required, to perform III.

2. The auditor must perform I, II, and III.

3. The auditor must perform I and II, but may not perform III.

4. The auditor may, but is not required to, perform I, II, and III.

---

4 Service Organizations

4.1 Effect on Internal Control

A service organization's services are considered to be part of a user entity's information system when such services affect the initiation, execution, processing, or reporting of the user's transactions.

4.2 Service Organization Reports

The service organization may issue one of two types of reports:

■ **Report on Controls Placed in Operation (Type 1 Report):** Helps the auditor understand controls.

■ **Report on Controls Placed in Operation and Tests of Operating Effectiveness (Type 2 Report):** Helps the auditor understand controls and may provide evidence supporting a reduction in the assessed level of control risk.

Question 3 MCQ-08111

Payroll Data Co. (PDC) processes payroll transactions for a retailer. Cook, CPA, is engaged to express an opinion on a description of PDC's internal controls placed in operation as of a specific date. These controls are relevant to the retailer's internal control, so Cook's report may be useful in providing the retailer's independent auditor with information necessary to plan a financial statement audit. Cook's report should:

1. Contain a disclaimer of opinion on the operating effectiveness of PDC's controls.

2. State whether PDC's controls were suitably designed to achieve the retailer's objectives.

3. Identify PDC's controls relevant to specific financial statement assertions.

4. Disclose Cook's assessed level of control risk for PDC.

---

5 The Effect of Information Technology (IT) on the Audit

A client's use of information technology affects both the evaluation of internal control and the gathering of evidence, but the audit objectives remain the same.

5.1 Evidence Gathering in an Automated Environment

An auditor can use manual audit procedures, e.g., "auditing around the computer," computer-assisted audit techniques (CAAT), e.g., "auditing through the computer," or a combination of the two.

5.1.1 Auditing Around the Computer

An auditor tests input data, processes data independently, and then compares the independent results to program results.

■ This is appropriate for simple batch systems with good audit trails.

■ The risks include insufficient paper-based evidence and insufficient audit procedures.

5.1.2 Auditing Through the Computer

■ **Transaction Tagging:** Electronically marks a transaction and allows the auditor to follow it through the client's system.

■ **Embedded Audit Modules:** An application program collects transaction data for the auditor. The auditor must be involved with the program design.

■ **Test Deck (Test Data):** Uses application program to process test data, the results of which are already known (client system, offline).

■ **Integrated Test Facility (ITF):** Test data is commingled with live data (client system, auditor's data, online).

■ **Parallel Simulation (Reperformance Test):** The auditor reprocesses some or all of the client's live data and compares the results with client files (auditor's system, client data).

■ **Generalized Audit Software Packages (GASP):** Allow the auditor to perform tests of controls and substantive tests directly on the client's system.

5.2 The Effect of Information Technology on Internal Control

Information technology use often affects an entity's internal control. IT brings increased risks but may also provide additional benefits.

5.2.1 IT Risks

- Potential reliance on inaccurate systems
- Loss of data and/or data inaccuracies from unauthorized data access
- Unauthorized changes to data, systems, or programs
- Failure to make required changes/updates to systems or programs

5.2.2 IT Benefits

- Accurate and consistent processing of large data/transaction volume
- Improved timeliness and availability of information
- Facilitation of data analysis and performance monitoring
- Reduction in the risk that controls will be circumvented
- Effective implementation of security controls enhances segregation of duties

Note

The accuracy of the IT system is crucial, because even manual controls may be dependent to some extent on the effective functioning of IT.

5.3 Assessing Control Risk

When assessing internal control, the auditor should consider the effects of both risks and benefits. Control risk assessment procedures in a computerized environment are the same as in manual systems (inquiry, inspection, observation, and reperformance).

5.4 The Effect of Information Technology on Audit Testing

- To select appropriate audit procedures, the auditor should consider the extent and complexity of the entity's computer operations, and the availability of an audit trail.

- Substantive tests alone may not suffice. Tests of controls should be performed to assess control risk in entities with significant computerized operations.

- The auditor needs to identify and test both specific application controls, and relevant general controls on which the application controls depend.

- The auditor should obtain an understanding of the internal control in effect throughout the period. Testing for operational integrity at a single point in time is generally not a reliable test of program controls. Although the auditor may make an initial assessment that a control is functioning as planned, subsequent testing is needed to ensure that the control continues to function effectively.

Question 4	MCQ-04383

An auditor most likely would introduce test data into a computerized payroll system to test internal controls related to the:

1. Existence of unclaimed payroll checks held by supervisors.
2. Early cashing of payroll checks by employees.
3. Discovery of invalid employee I.D. numbers.
4. Proper approval of overtime by supervisors.

Question 5   MCQ-08126

When an auditor tests a computerized accounting system, which of the following is true of the test data approach?

1. Several transactions of each type must be tested.

2. Test data are processed by the client's computer programs under the auditor's control.

3. Test data must consist of all possible valid and invalid conditions.

4. The program tested is different from the program used throughout the year by the client.

1 Auditor Responsibility

The auditor must obtain reasonable assurance about whether the financial statements are free of material misstatements, whether caused by error or fraud.

1.1 Error

Error is an unintentional misstatement or omission.

1.2 Fraud

Fraud is an intentional misstatement or omission in the financial statements. Fraud often involves management because management is in a position to manipulate, directly or indirectly, accounting records. Management also can override established controls.

Question 1   MCQ-09030

The auditor's responsibility regarding material misstatements caused by *fraud* is:

1. Less than the auditor's responsibility regarding material misstatements caused by *error*.

2. Greater than the auditor's responsibility regarding material misstatements caused by *error*.

3. The same as the auditor's responsibility regarding material misstatements caused by *error*.

4. Either less than or greater than the auditor's responsibility regarding material misstatements caused by *error*, depending on the specific circumstances.

---

2 Categories of Fraud

Fraud is divided into two categories:

2.1 Fraudulent Financial Reporting

Intentional misstatements or omissions of amounts/disclosures in the financial statements; committed by management with the intent to deceive.

2.2 Misappropriation of Assets (Defalcation)

Theft of an entity's assets; committed by management, employees, or third parties.

3 Presumed Fraud Risk

There is a presumption in every audit that the following two risks exist:

- Improper revenue recognition
- Management override of controls

4 Fraud Risk Factors

Three conditions generally are present when fraud occurs:

- **Incentives/Pressures:** A reason to commit fraud.
- **Opportunity:** Ineffective controls or override of controls.
- **Rationalization/Attitude:** Justification of fraudulent behavior.

Question 2

MCQ-09037

Which of the following is *not* true regarding fraud risk factors?

1. They include incentives/pressures, opportunity, and rationalization.
2. Lack of observation of the three fraud risk factors implies that there is no fraud risk.
3. The existence of all three fraud risk factors is not an absolute indication that fraud has occurred.
4. Fraud risk factors are often present in circumstances where fraud has occurred.

5 Audit Procedures to Address Fraud Risk

The auditor must exercise professional skepticism throughout the audit process.

- Discuss fraud risk with engagement personnel.
- Obtain information to identify specific fraud risks.
- Assess fraud risk and develop an appropriate response.
- Evaluate audit evidence regarding fraud.
- Make appropriate communications about fraud.
- Document the auditor's consideration of fraud.

Question 3

MCQ-09818

Which of the following items is *not* required to be documented about the required fraud brainstorming session?

1. The auditor's responsibility to provide absolute assurance to uncover fraud.
2. The audit team members who participated.
3. How and when the discussion occurred.
4. Significant decisions reached.

6 Communication of Fraud

6.1 To Management and Those Charged With Governance

Fraud that causes a material financial statement misstatement should always be reported directly to management and those charged with governance.

- Obtain sufficient evidence of fraud and its effects on the financial statements.
- Discuss with an appropriate level of management at least one level higher than where fraud occurred.
- Suggest that client consult with legal counsel.

6.2 To Third Parties

Ordinarily, the auditor does not disclose fraud to third parties. However, in certain circumstances a duty to disclose to outsiders may exist:

- to the SEC in order to comply with certain legal and regulatory requirements, such as on Form 8-K and other required reports.
- to a successor auditor when they make inquiries.
- in a response to subpoena.
- to a funding agency that receives governmental financial assistance.

1 Audit Risk (AR)

AR is the risk that the auditor may unknowingly fail to modify appropriately the opinion on materially misstated financial statements. The auditor should plan the audit so that overall audit risk is limited to a low level. AR includes:

1.1 Risk of Material Misstatement (RMM)

The risk that the financial statements are materially misstated. It can be subdivided into:

1.1.1 Inherent Risk (IR)

Susceptibility of an assertion to a material misstatement assuming that there are no related controls.

- IR exists independently of the audit.
- The auditor cannot change this risk.

1.1.2 Control Risk (CR)

The risk that a material misstatement could occur in an assertion and not be prevented or detected on a timely basis by an entity's internal control.

- CR exists independently of the audit.
- The auditor cannot change this risk, but can change his/her assessment of the risk based on evidence gathered during the audit.
- The stronger the system of controls, the greater the reliance that may be placed on it, and the fewer the substantive tests (or the lower the quality) required.

1.2 Detection Risk (DR)

The risk that the auditor will not detect a material misstatement that exists in an assertion. DR relates to the auditor's procedures.

- The auditor can change this risk by varying the nature, extent, or timing of audit procedures.
- As the acceptable level of DR decreases, the assurance provided from substantive tests should increase.

1.3 The Audit Risk Model

| Audit risk (AR) | = | Risk of material misstatement (RMM) (assessed by auditor) | × | Detection risk (DR) (controlled by auditor) |

Risk of Material Misstatement	Acceptable Level of Detection Risk	Determine "NET" of Substantive Tests
High ↑ (Bad)	Lower ↓	High ↑
Low ↓ (Good)	Higher ↑	Low ↓

Question 1   MCQ-08828

After making a preliminary assessment of the risk of material misstatement during planning and beginning to apply audit procedures, an auditor determines that this risk is actually higher than anticipated. Which would be the *most likely* effect of this finding on the auditor's desired level of detection risk and the overall level of audit risk, as compared to the levels originally planned?

	Auditor's Desired Level of Detection Risk	*Overall Level of Audit Risk*
1.	Decrease	Same
2.	Increase	Same
3.	Same	Higher
4.	Decrease	Lower

Question 2   MCQ-09815

As the acceptable level of detection risk increases, an auditor may:

1. Change the nature of substantive tests from a less effective to a more effective procedure.

2. Postpone the planned timing of substantive tests from interim dates to year-end.

3. Lower the assessed level of inherent risk.

4. Select a smaller sample size.

2 Procedures

2.1 Overview

The auditor must perform the following procedures in order to assess and respond to risk:

- Obtain an understanding of the entity and its environment, including its internal control.
- Assess the risk of material misstatement.
- Respond to the assessed level of risk by performing further audit procedures (tests of controls and substantive tests).
- Evaluate audit evidence.

2.2 Obtaining an Understanding

The auditor should understand:

- Industry, regulatory, and other external factors.
- The nature of the entity.
- The entity's objectives, strategies, and business risks.
- The entity's financial performance.
- The entity's internal control:
  - includes evaluating the design of controls and determining whether they have been implemented.
  - does not require an evaluation of the operating effectiveness of controls (but the auditor may purposefully or incidentally obtain evidence about operating effectiveness at this time).
- Under PCAOB standards, the auditor of an issuer must also obtain an understanding of the company's selection and application of accounting principles.

2.3 Risk Assessment Procedures

The understanding is obtained by performing the following risk assessment procedures:

- Inquiry
- Analytical procedures
- Audit data analytics
- Observation and inspection
- Audit team discussion

Question 3   MCQ-09029

Analytical procedures used in planning an audit should focus on:

1. Reducing the scope of tests of controls and substantive tests.
2. Providing assurance that potential material misstatements will be identified.
3. Enhancing the auditor's understanding of the client's business.
4. Assessing the adequacy of the available audit evidence.

Question 4   MCQ-09817

Which one of the following is a true statement about the required risk assessment discussion?

1. The discussion about the susceptibility of the entity's financial statements to material misstatement must be held separately from the discussion about the susceptibility of the entity's financial statements to fraud.
2. The discussion should involve all members who participate on the audit team, including the engagement partner.
3. The discussion should include consideration of the risk of management override of controls.
4. The risk assessment discussion should occur during the overall review stage of the audit.

1 Management Assertions (**COVERU**)

Management makes assertions about transactions and events, account balances, and presentation and disclosure.

1.1 Main Assertions

There are six main financial statement assertions (Note that under PCAOB standards, the main financial statement assertions are completeness; valuation or allocation; existence and occurrence; rights and obligations; and presentation and disclosure):

1.1.1 Completeness

All account balances, transactions, and disclosures that should have been recorded have been recorded and included in the financial statements.

1.1.2 Cutoff

Transactions have been recorded in the correct (proper) accounting period.

1.1.3 Valuation, Allocation, and Accuracy

Account balances, transactions, and disclosures are recorded fairly and at appropriate amounts, and any resulting valuation or allocation adjustments are appropriately recorded.

1.1.4 Existence and Occurrence

Account balances exist and transactions that have been recorded and disclosed have occurred and pertain to the entity.

1.1.5 Rights and Obligations

The entity holds or controls the rights to assets, and liabilities are the obligations of the entity.

1.1.6 Understandability and Classification

Transactions have been recorded in the proper accounts. Financial information is appropriately presented and described and disclosures are clearly expressed.

1.2 Relevant Assertions

Relevant assertions are assertions that have a meaningful bearing on whether an account, transaction, or disclosure is fairly stated.

1.2.1 Transactions and Events

For transactions and events, relevant assertions include completeness, cutoff, accuracy, classification, and occurrence.

1.2.2 Account Balances

For account balances, relevant assertions include completeness, allocation and valuation, rights and obligations, and existence.

1.2.3 Presentation and Disclosure

For presentation and disclosure, relevant assertions include completeness, understandability and classification, rights and obligations, and valuation and accuracy.

Question 1   MCQ-08123

In assessing control risk for purchases, an auditor vouches a sample of entries in the voucher register to the supporting documents. Which assertion would this test of controls most likely support?

1. Completeness.

2. Occurrence.

3. Allocation and valuation.

4. Rights and obligations.

Question 2   MCQ-09066

An auditor wishes to test the completeness assertion for sales. Which of the following audit tests would most likely accomplish this objective?

1. Select a sample of shipments occurring during the year and trace each one to inclusion in the sales journal.

2. Compare accounts receivable turnover (net credit sales / average gross receivables) in the current year to that achieved in the prior year.

3. Use common size analysis to compare recorded sales to sales recorded by other companies in the same industry.

4. Select large individual sales recorded during the year and review supporting documentation.

---

2 Assessing Risk

The auditor should:

■ Identify and assess specific risks at the assertion level and at the financial statement level.

■ Give special consideration to significant risks.

■ Identify relevant controls.

■ Document the following:

- Key elements of the understanding of the entity and its environment, including the components of internal control

- Identified risks and related controls

- Risk assessment procedures performed

- The auditor's risk assessment and the basis for this assessment

---

Question 3   MCQ-09806

Which of the following documentation is *not* required for an audit in accordance with generally accepted auditing standards?

1. A written audit plan setting forth the procedures necessary to accomplish the audit objectives.

2. The basis for the auditor's decision to perform tests of controls concurrently with obtaining an understanding of internal control.

3. The auditor's understanding of the entity's control activities that help ensure achievement of management's objectives.

4. The assessment of the risks of material misstatement at both the financial statement and relevant assertion levels.

Notes

1 Levels of Response

1.1 Overall Response

Overall responses to an assessed high risk of material misstatement include:

- Communicate to the audit team an increased need for professional skepticism.
- Assign staff with more experience or specialized skills.
- Increase the level of supervision.
- Incorporate a greater level of unpredictability into the audit.
- Make changes to the nature, extent, and timing of tests.

1.2 Assertion Level Response

There should be a clear linkage between the assessed level of risk at the relevant assertion level and the nature, extent, and timing of further audit procedures, including tests of controls and substantive procedures.

1.3 Response to Significant Risks

If relying on the operating effectiveness of internal controls intended to mitigate significant risk, tests of controls must be performed in the current period. Substantive procedures can consist of tests of details only, or tests of details and substantive analytical procedures.

Question 1 — MCQ-09865

Which of the following represents an appropriate overall response to an increase in financial statement level risk?

1. Providing management with more specific details about audit sampling procedures.
2. Changing the general approach of the audit to ensure control testing of all significant accounts.
3. Shifting substantive procedures to interim.
4. Increasing the level of supervision.

---

2 Further Audit Procedures

Based on assessed risk at the relevant assertion level, the auditor designs the nature, extent, and timing of further audit procedures.

- **Nature:** the purpose and type of test.
- **Extent:** the quantity of testing.
- **Timing:** interim or period end.

3 Audit Approaches

3.1 Substantive Approach

Under a substantive approach, only substantive procedures are performed.

3.2 Combined Approach

Under a combined approach, tests of the operating effectiveness of controls and substantive procedures (perhaps at a reduced level) are both performed. In a combined approach, the nature, extent, and timing of substantive testing is affected by the operating effectiveness of controls:

- The more effective a control, the lower the assessed level of control risk (CR). As CR decreases, the acceptable level of detection risk (DR) increases and the assurance required from substantive tests decreases.
- Conversely, as the acceptable level of DR decreases, the assurance that must be obtained from substantive tests increases.
- The stronger a control, the more it can be relied upon, and the fewer the required substantive tests (or the lower the quality).

When Do We Test Controls?		
Status of Controls	*Risk Level*	*Audit Work*
No controls	Maximum Risk	Do not test controls*
Weak controls	High Risk	Do not test controls*
Some controls	Moderate Risk	Test the controls
Strong controls	Low Risk	Test the controls

* Exception: If significant electronic processing is used, controls should be tested.

Question 2   MCQ-08320

Using a combined approach most likely would involve:

1. Performing more extensive substantive tests with larger sample sizes than originally planned.

2. Reducing inherent risk for most of the assertions relevant to significant account balances.

3. Changing the timing of substantive tests by omitting interim-date testing and performing the tests at year-end.

4. Identifying specific internal controls relevant to specific assertions.

1 Materiality

Materiality is the amount of error or omission that would affect the judgment of a reasonable person. The auditor should make preliminary assessments of materiality and should revise those assessments as appropriate throughout the audit.

1.1 Materiality for the Financial Statements as a Whole

Materiality for the financial statements as a whole needs to be expressed as a specific amount.

- Materiality should be based on the smallest level of misstatement that could be material to any one of the financial statements.
- Both qualitative and quantitative factors should be used to assess materiality, including:
  - The application of a percentage to an appropriate financial statement benchmark
  - Prior period and current period financial results
  - Known or expected changes in the entity's circumstances, the industry, or the economy

1.2 Performance Materiality

Performance materiality consists of the amount(s) set at less than materiality for the financial statements as a whole in order to reduce to an appropriately low level the probability that the aggregate of uncorrected and undetected misstatements exceeds the materiality for the financial statements as a whole.

1.3 Tolerable Misstatement

Tolerable misstatement is the application of performance materiality to a particular sampling procedure.

1.4 Materiality for Classes of Transactions, Account Balances, or Disclosures

A separate materiality level should be set for a particular class of transactions, account balances, or disclosures when misstatements of an amount less than materiality for the financial statements as a whole could influence the economic decisions of users.

Question 1   MCQ-09800

In which of the following circumstances would an auditor of an issuer be *least likely* to reevaluate established materiality levels?

1. The materiality level was established based on preliminary financial statement amounts that differ significantly from actual amounts.

2. The client disposed a major portion of the client's business.

3. The client released third-quarter results before the SEC-prescribed deadline.

4. Significant new contractual arrangements draw attention to a particular aspect of a client's business that is separately disclosed in the financial statements.

1 Internal Audit Function

Independent auditors cannot share responsibility for audit decisions, assessments, or for issuing the report with a client's internal auditor. However, the internal auditor may assist with routine tasks.

1.1 Critical Factors

An auditor wishing to make use of an internal auditor's work must consider critical factors, including:

- The competence of the internal audit function, as evidenced by education, professional certification, and the quality of internal audit documentation.

- The objectivity of the internal auditors, based on the organizational level to which the internal audit function reports.

- The application of a systematic and disciplined approach, as evidenced by the use of documented internal audit procedures and quality control policies.

Question 1 — MCQ-08139

In assessing the competence and objectivity of an entity's internal auditor, an independent auditor would *least likely* consider information obtained from:

1. Discussions with management personnel.

2. External quality reviews of the internal auditor's work.

3. Previous experience with the internal auditor.

4. The results of analytical procedures.

---

2 Use of Specialists

Actuaries, appraisers, attorneys, and engineers (specialists) may be used to assist the auditor in considering valuation or complex transactions. The auditor should understand the specialist's field of expertise, competence, capabilities, and objectivity to determine the possibility of using the specialist's work.

2.1   Impact on Audit Report

If, as a result of the work performed by the specialist, the auditor decides to add explanatory language or depart from an unqualified opinion, the auditor may refer to the specialist in the report and should indicate that the reference to the specialist does not reduce the auditor's responsibility for the audit opinion. In addition, an auditor of an issuer may reference the specialist if it helps the users understand a critical audit matter. The auditor may need the permission of the specialist before making reference to the specialist.

Question 2   MCQ-09802

Which of the following procedures is the auditor *least likely* to perform when an auditor decides to use the work of an auditor's specialist as audit evidence?

1. Obtain knowledge of the specialist's qualifications.

2. Refer to the auditor's specialist in the audit report to indicate a division of responsibility.

3. Inquire of the entity and the auditor's specialist about any known interests that the entity has with the auditor's external specialist that may affect that specialist's objectivity.

4. Review the working papers of the auditor's specialist.

---

1 Related Party Transactions

1.1 Auditor Responsibility

Throughout the audit process, the auditor must be alert for the existence of transactions with related parties, such as entity affiliates, principal owners, management, and members of their immediate families. The auditor's primary concern with respect to related party transactions is their proper disclosure in accordance with GAAP.

1.2 Audit Procedures

Specific procedures regarding material transactions with related parties may include:

- Evaluation of the company's procedures to identify and account for related party transactions.

- Inquiry of management regarding the names of all related parties.

- Review of the reporting entity's filings with the SEC and other regulatory agencies concerning the names of officers and directors who occupy management or directorship positions in other businesses.

- Review of material transactions for related party evidence.

Question 1   MCQ-09074

Which of the following auditing procedures most likely would assist an auditor in identifying related party transactions?

1. Inspecting correspondence with lawyers for evidence of unreported contingent liabilities.

2. Vouching accounting records for recurring transactions recorded just after the balance sheet date.

3. Reviewing confirmations of loans receivable and payable for indications of guarantees.

4. Performing analytical procedures for indications of possible financial difficulties.

---

2 Noncompliance With Laws and Regulations

2.1 Noncompliance

Noncompliance is an act of omission or commission by an entity, whether intentional or unintentional, which is contrary to prevailing laws and regulations.

2.2 Management's Responsibility

Management and those charged with governance are responsible for ensuring that the entity's operations are conducted in accordance with applicable laws and regulations.

2.3 Auditor's Responsibility

The auditor is responsible for obtaining reasonable assurance that the financial statements are free of material misstatement due to noncompliance with laws and regulations.

- The auditor is not responsible for preventing noncompliance and cannot be expected to detect noncompliance with all laws and regulations.
- The further removed noncompliance is from the financial statements, the less likely the auditor is to recognize the noncompliance.

2.4 Procedures When Noncompliance Is Identified or Suspected

If the auditor suspects that noncompliance may exist, the auditor should discuss the matter with management at least one level above those suspected of noncompliance and, when appropriate, those charged with governance.

2.5 Reporting Noncompliance in the Auditor's Report

2.5.1 Material Effect on the Financial Statements

If the noncompliance has a material effect on the financial statements and has not been adequately reflected in the financial statements, a qualified opinion or adverse opinion should be issued.

2.5.2 Insufficient Evidence

If the auditor is unable to obtain sufficient appropriate audit evidence about the noncompliance or suspected noncompliance, a qualified opinion or a disclaimer of opinion should be expressed.

2.5.3 Client Response

If the client refuses to accept the auditor's report as modified, the auditor should withdraw from the engagement and notify those charged with governance in writing.

Question 2   MCQ-09822

Which of the following information discovered during an audit most likely would raise a question concerning possible noncompliance with laws and regulations?

1. A piece of obsolete office equipment was not retired.

2. Material internal control weaknesses previously reported to management were not corrected.

3. The client receives financial assistance from a federal government agency.

4. There was an illegal payment to a foreign official.

---

1 Fair Value Measurements

- Management is responsible for making fair value measurements and disclosures in accordance with GAAP.

- The auditor tests such measurements and disclosures to provide reasonable assurance that they are in conformity with GAAP.

2 Accounting Estimates

The auditor should verify that:

- Appropriate practices are used to develop estimates.
- All material estimates are reasonable.
- Estimates are presented in conformity with GAAP.
- Estimates are properly disclosed.

Question 1   MCQ-08121

Which of the following best describes the auditor's responsibility with respect to fair values?

1. The auditor should determine whether management has the intent and ability to carry out courses of action that may affect fair values.

2. The auditor should assess the risk of material misstatement of fair value measurements.

3. The auditor should obtain sufficient competent audit evidence to provide reasonable assurance that fair value measurements and disclosures are in conformity with GAAP.

4. The auditor should make fair value measurements and disclosures in accordance with GAAP and should identify and support any significant assumptions used.

Question 2   MCQ-09065

With respect to accounting estimates, an auditor:

1. Is not responsible for auditing estimated amounts, since they may be based on subjective determinations made by management.

2. Should verify that all material estimates required by generally accepted accounting principles have been developed.

3. Should focus on assumptions that are objective, insensitive to variation, and don't deviate from historical patterns.

4. Bears responsibility for making reasonable estimates and including them in the financial statements.

III Performing Further Procedures and Obtaining Evidence

1 Audit Evidence

Evidence consists of underlying accounting data and corroborating evidence. Evidence must be sufficient and appropriate to afford a reasonable basis for an opinion regarding the assertions in the financial statements.

1.1 Sufficient Audit Evidence

The auditor must use professional judgment to determine the amounts and kinds of evidence sufficient to support an opinion. Sufficiency is influenced by:

- The risk of material misstatement (More risk = More evidence)
- The quality of the audit evidence (Low quality = More evidence)

1.2 Appropriate Audit Evidence

Appropriate audit evidence must be both reliable and relevant. Appropriateness depends on being pertinent, objective, timely, and corroborated.

1.2.1 Reliability

Reliability is dependent on the circumstances under which evidence is gathered. From most reliable to least reliable:

- Auditor's direct personal knowledge and observation
- External evidence
- Internal evidence
- Oral evidence

1.2.2 Relevance

Relevance means the evidence is related to (i.e., tells something about) the assertion under consideration. PCAOB standards state that the relevance of evidence depends on the design of the audit procedure (whether it is designed to test the assertion directly or whether it is designed to test for overstatement or understatement) and the timing of the audit procedure.

Question 1   MCQ-09858

Which of the following circumstances most likely would cause an auditor to suspect that there are material misstatements in an entity's financial statements?

1. The entity's management strictly enforces its integrity and ethical values.

2. Monthly bank reconciliations ordinarily include several outstanding checks.

3. Management outsources the internal audit function to another CPA firm.

4. The auditor identifies an inappropriate valuation method that is widely applied by the entity.

Sampling Techniques

1 Statistical and Nonstatistical Sampling

Sampling can be statistical (mathematical) or nonstatistical. Both can provide sufficient audit evidence and are acceptable under GAAS; both require professional judgment. Only statistical sampling enables the auditor to measure the sufficiency of the evidence, design an efficient sample, and quantify sampling risk.

2 Types of Statistical Sampling

2.1 Attribute Sampling

Attributes sampling is used to estimate a rate of occurrence (whether or not an attribute is present); primarily used to test internal controls. Methods include:

- Discovery sampling
- Stop and go sampling
- Acceptance sampling

2.2 Variables Sampling

Variables sampling is used to estimate numerical value; typically used in substantive testing. The auditor estimates a population's true value by computing a point estimate of the population and a precision interval around the estimate. Methods include:

- Mean-per-unit estimation (MPU)
- Ratio estimation
- Difference estimation

2.2.1 PPS Sampling

Probability-proportional-to-size (PPS) sampling is a hybrid method that uses attribute sampling theory to express a conclusion in dollar amounts.

Question 1   MCQ-08135

An advantage of using statistical over nonstatistical sampling methods in tests of controls is that the statistical methods:

1. Can more easily convert the sample into a dual-purpose test useful for substantive testing.

2. Eliminate the need to use judgment in determining appropriate sample sizes.

3. Afford greater assurance than a nonstatistical sample of equal size.

4. Provide an objective basis for quantitatively evaluating sample risk.

Question 2   MCQ-09024

An auditor is likely using attribute sampling when he or she selects a sample of:

1. Receivables and sends confirmations to client customers.

2. Purchase orders and examines them for indication of proper approval.

3. Invoices to verify proper extensions and footings.

4. Cash receipts and traces them to the accounts receivable subsidiary ledger.

3 Sampling Risk

Sampling risk is the risk that the sample is not representative, and that the auditor's conclusion would be different from the conclusion if the auditor had examined 100 percent of the population.

3.1 Confidence Interval

Numerically, sampling risk is the complement of reliability, or confidence level (e.g., a 5 percent sampling risk reflects a 95 percent confidence level).

3.2 Sampling Risks in Tests of Controls (Attribute Sampling)

3.2.1 Risk of Assessing Control Risk Too Low

The risk of assessing control risk too low is the risk that a properly drawn sample will support the auditor's planned degree of reliance when the true compliance rate does not justify such reliance (risk of overreliance).

3.2.2 Risk of Assessing Control Risk Too High

The risk of assessing control risk too high is the risk that a properly drawn sample will not support the auditor's planned degree of reliance when the true compliance rate does justify such reliance (risk of under-reliance).

Diagram 1: Attribute Sampling Risks

The true operation of the control is:

		OK	Not OK
The sample indicates that the operation of the control is:	OK	Correct decision	Incorrect decision **Risk of assessing control risk too low** *Not effective*
	Not OK	Incorrect decision **Risk of assessing control risk too high** *Not efficient*	Correct decision

3.3 Sampling Risks in Substantive Testing (Variables Sampling)

3.3.1 Risk of Incorrect Acceptance

The risk of incorrect acceptance is the risk that a properly drawn sample supports a balance as not being materially misstated when in fact it is materially misstated.

3.3.2 Risk of Incorrect Rejection

The risk of incorrect rejection is the risk that a properly drawn sample supports a balance as materially misstated when in fact it is not materially misstated.

Diagram 2: Variables Sampling Risks

		The recorded value of the population is:	
		OK	**Not OK**
The sample indicates that the population is:	**OK**	Correct decision	Incorrect decision **Risk of incorrect acceptance** *Not effective*
	Not OK	Incorrect decision **Risk of incorrect rejection** *Not efficient*	Correct decision

---

3.4 Effect of Sampling Risk on the Audit

3.4.1 Effectiveness

The risk of assessing control risk too low and the risk of incorrect acceptance are concerned with the effectiveness of the audit. This type of risk is more critical because it can result in the auditor mistakenly relying on an ineffective control or unknowingly accepting a misstatement in the balance being tested and thereby issuing an inappropriate audit opinion.

3.4.2 Efficiency

The risk of assessing control risk too high and the risk of incorrect rejection are concerned with the efficiency of the audit. An audit conclusion in this direction causes the auditor to do more work than is really necessary.

Question 3   MCQ-04494

In assessing sampling risk, the risk of incorrect rejection and the risk of assessing control risk too high relate to the:

1. Efficiency of the audit.
2. Effectiveness of the audit.
3. Selection of the items in the sample.
4. Audit quality controls.

---

4 Steps in the Sampling Process

Attribute Sampling	Variables Sampling
1. Define the objective: This is the purpose of the test.	
Percentage of sales orders missing credit approval (i.e., what is the percentage of control failure).	True dollar value of sales for year 20X5.
2. Define the population: This is the aggregate group or set of items about which the auditor wishes to draw conclusions.	
All new customer sales orders during 20X5.	All sales dollars for year 20X5.
3. Define the sampling unit: This is the actual item or element from which the auditor will collect data.	
Individual sales orders.	Individual sales dollars.
4. Define the attribute of interest: This is the data to be collected.	
Credit approval (e.g., manager's signature). Missing approvals or missing sales orders are deviations.	Sales dollars.
5. Determine the sample size: This is the number of items to be selected for testing. The decision is based on statistical considerations, plus the auditor's judgment.	
Sample size is affected by the risk of assessing control risk too low (inverse relationship), the tolerable deviation rate (inverse), and the expected deviation rate (direct). Population size (>5000 items) generally does not matter.	Sample size is affected by expected misstatement, standard deviation, and the assessed level of risk (direct effects), as well as by tolerable misstatement and the acceptable level of risk (inverse effects).
6. Select the sample: The actual selection of a representative set of items for testing.	
Random selection: Best method (used with prenumbered population). *Systematic selection*: Every nth item (ineffective if population is systematically ordered). *Stratification*: Divide the population into subpopulations based on strata. *Block or cluster*: Not a desirable approach. *PPS*: Every nth dollar, uses a random start, automatically stratifies population but does not test negative or zero balances.	
7. Evaluate the sample results: This tells the auditor if the control can be relied on (attribute sampling) or if the account does not appear to be materially misstated (variables sampling).	
Compare upper deviation rate to tolerable deviation rate. Sample deviation rate + Allowance for sampling risk = **Upper deviation rate** **Tolerable deviation rate:** maximum rate of deviation from prescribed controls that the auditor will tolerate without modifying planned reliance on the control. (Based on professional judgment.) **Sample deviation rate:** error rate in the sample; the auditor's best estimate of the deviation rate in the population from which the sample was selected.	Auditor projects misstatements to population utilizing a projected misstatement (point estimate). An allowance for sampling risk (or precision interval) is added to this estimate. Sample error + recorded balance = point estimate Form conclusions about the account balances/transactions tested: Accept book value if it falls within an acceptable range (point estimate +/− allowance for sampling risk). Likely misstatement = Projected misstatement **Tolerable misstatement:** misstatement in the related account balance or class of transactions that may exist without causing the FS to be materially misstated.
8. Document sampling procedures.	

Question 4 | MCQ-08117

A number of factors influence the sample size for a substantive test of details of an account balance. All other factors being equal, which of the following would lead to a larger sample size?

1. Greater reliance on internal control.

2. Greater reliance on analytical procedures.

3. Smaller expected frequency of errors.

4. Smaller measure of tolerable misstatement.

---

5 Example of Evaluating Sample Results for Attribute Sampling

- Sample deviation rate = (Number of errors)/(Sample size)

  10 errors / 1000 sample size = 1%

- Sample deviation rate + Allowance for sampling risk = Upper deviation rate

  1.0% + 3.7% = 4.7%

- Compare upper deviation rate (UDR) to tolerable rate (TR).

  UDR ≤ TR   Assume TR = 6.0%

  No change in preliminary assessment of control risk is needed

  No change in NET of substantive tests is needed

  4.7% < 6.0% would be a "good" result

  UDR > TR   Assume TR = 3.0%

  Increase the assessment of control risk, resulting in a change in NET of substantive tests:

  Nature: Select a more effective substantive test.

  Extent: Increase the substantive test sample size.

  Timing: Apply substantive tests at year-end instead of at interim.

  4.7% > 3.0% would be a "bad" result

Question 5

An auditor who uses statistical sampling for attributes in testing internal controls should reduce the planned reliance on a prescribed control when the:

1. Sample rate of deviation plus the allowance for sampling risk equals the tolerable rate.

2. Sample rate of deviation is less than the expected rate of deviation used in planning the sample.

3. Tolerable rate less the allowance for sampling risk exceeds the sample rate of deviation.

4. Sample rate of deviation plus the allowance for sampling risk exceeds the tolerable rate.

6 Probability-Proportional-to-Size (PPS) Sampling

Under PPS sampling, the sampling unit is defined as an individual dollar in a population. Once the dollar is selected, the entire account is audited.

6.1 Advantage

Automatically emphasizes larger items, so if no errors are expected, PPS will require a smaller sample than other methods.

6.2 Disadvantage

Zero balances, negative balances, and understated balances generally require special design considerations.

6.3 Steps in PPS Sampling

- Sample size = recorded amount of the population/sampling interval.

- Sampling interval = tolerable misstatement/reliability factor.

- Reliability factors correspond to the risk of incorrect acceptance and are generally obtained from a table.

- **Sample Selection:** A random number between 1 and the sampling interval is selected; it determines the first item selected. The recorded amounts of the logical units throughout the population are then added and individual dollars (and their corresponding units) are selected based on the interval.

- **Evaluation of Sample Results:** If no errors are found, the error projection is zero and the allowance for sampling risk would not exceed the auditor's tolerable error. If errors are found, they need to be projected to the interval. If an account selected has a balance greater than the interval, the actual dollar amount of the error should be used.

Probability-Proportional-to-Size							
	A Recorded Amount	B Audit Amount	A–B	A	(A–B)/A Tainting	Sample Interval	Projected Error
	$800	$600	$200	$800	25%	$5,000	$1,250
	4,350	4,350	0	4,350	0%	5,000	0
	4,900	0	4,900	4,900	100%	5,000	5,000
> 5,000	8,500	6,900	1,600	n/a	n/a	n/a	1,600
	<u>1,500</u>	<u>1,200</u>	<u>300</u>	1,500	20%	5,000	<u>1,000</u>
Totals	20,050	13,050	7,000				8,850

Known misstatement (sample errors)	7,000
Projected error	8,850
Allowance for sampling risk (calculation not shown)	<u>2,500</u>
Projected misstatement (likely misstatement)	11,350

If tolerable misstatement is 15,000, the book value is fairly stated (11,350 is less than 15,000)

7 Dual Purpose Samples

Auditors may use the same sample to perform both tests of controls and substantive tests; generally this would only be done when the auditor believes that there is an acceptably low risk that the deviation rate in the population exceeds the tolerable rate.

In evaluating dual-purpose samples, deviations from control procedures and monetary misstatements should be evaluated separately using appropriate risk levels.

1 Purpose

Tests of controls are used to evaluate the operating effectiveness of internal control in preventing or detecting material misstatements. Tests of controls are necessary when:

- The risk assessment is based on the operating effectiveness of internal control.
- Substantive procedures alone are insufficient because there is extensive use of information technology.

2 Tests of Operating Effectiveness

Testing the operating effectiveness of internal controls includes obtaining evidence regarding:

- Whether the controls were applied at relevant times
- How the controls were applied
- The consistency with which the controls were applied
- By whom or by what means the controls were applied

3 Nature, Extent, and Timing

3.1 Nature

The auditor should use a combination of procedures to obtain sufficient evidence of operating effectiveness. Acceptable procedures include:

- Reperformance
- Inspection
- Observation
- Inquiry

3.2 Extent

The auditor should consider the following factors to determine the extent of a control test:

■ Frequency of performance of control

■ Length of time over which the auditor intends to rely on the control

■ Relevance and reliability of the evidence

■ The extent to which other tests provide evidence about the assertion

■ The extent to which the auditor intends to rely on the operating effectiveness of the control to reduce substantive procedures

■ Expected deviation rate

3.3 Timing

Controls tested at a point in time provide evidence that the control operated effectively at that time, whereas controls tested throughout the period provide evidence of the operating effectiveness during the period.

4 Results

After performing tests of controls, the auditor may conclude that audit evidence indicates that:

■ controls are operating effectively and can be relied upon.

■ controls are not operating effectively, in which case the auditor can:

• test alternative controls; or

• respond to the assessed risk of material misstatement with more reliable and extensive substantive procedures.

Question 1 MCQ-08113

Which of the following is *least* likely to be evidence the auditor examines to determine whether controls are operating effectively?

   1. Records documenting usage of computer programs.

   2. Canceled supporting documents.

   3. Confirmations of accounts receivable.

   4. Signatures on authorization forms.

---

1 Use of Analytical Procedures in the Audit

Analytical procedures are evaluations of financial information made by a study of plausible relationships between financial and nonfinancial data.

1.1 Types of Analytical Procedures

Analytical procedures generally involve comparisons of recorded amounts to independent expectations developed by the auditor, including:

- Comparisons of financial data, such as comparison of current and prior year financial statements
- Ratio analysis

1.2 Use During the Audit

Analytical procedures are used during the planning, substantive procedure, and final review stages of the audit.

Phase	Requirement	Purpose
Planning	Required	To assist the auditor in understanding the entity and its environment. Used for risk measurement to alert the auditor to problem areas requiring attention. This serves a vital planning function.
Substantive procedures	Not required	As a substantive test to obtain audit evidence about specific management assertions related to account balances or transactions. The evidence is circumstantial and generally additional corroborating evidence (such as documentation) must be obtained.
Final review	Required	To assist the auditor in the final review of the overall reasonableness of account balances.

Question 1   MCQ-09856

An auditor notices that interest expense stayed approximately the same as the prior year even though the debt outstanding significantly increased from the prior year. The client only invests in debt that has a fixed interest rate. Which of the following best explains the reason for the above explanation?

    1. The company paid off a significant portion of the debt.

    2. The company acquired a new loan for construction of a building that began during the year under audit.

    3. The Federal Reserve decreased interest rates in the current year.

    4. The company acquired a new loan at midyear related to the acquisition of a competitor.

2   Ratio Analysis

2.1   Liquidity Ratios

Measures of a firm's short-term ability to pay maturing obligations.

$$\text{Working capital} = \text{Current assets} - \text{Current liabilities}$$

$$\text{Current ratio (working capital ratio)} = \frac{\text{Current assets}}{\text{Current liabilities}}$$

$$\text{Quick ratio} = \frac{\text{Cash and cash equivalents} + \text{Short-term marketable securities} + \text{Accounts receivable (net)}}{\text{Current liabilities}}$$

■ Generally, as the current/quick ratios increase, an entity's ability to meet short-term obligation improves (and vice versa).

2.2 Activity Ratios

Measures of how effectively an enterprise is using its assets.

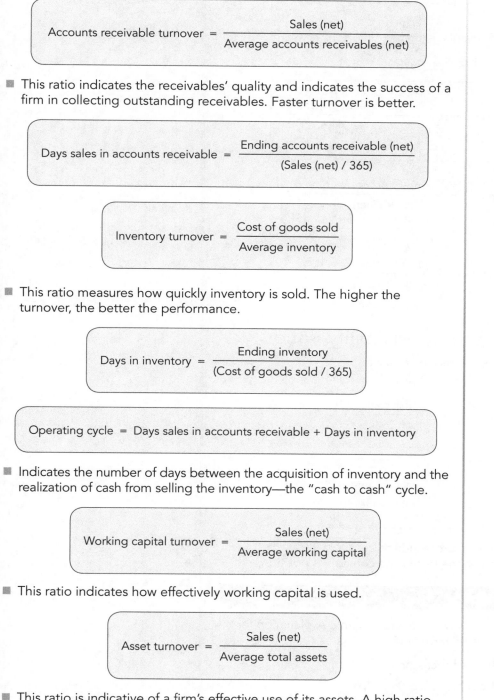

$$\text{Accounts receivable turnover} = \frac{\text{Sales (net)}}{\text{Average accounts receivables (net)}}$$

- This ratio indicates the receivables' quality and indicates the success of a firm in collecting outstanding receivables. Faster turnover is better.

$$\text{Days sales in accounts receivable} = \frac{\text{Ending accounts receivable (net)}}{\text{(Sales (net) / 365)}}$$

$$\text{Inventory turnover} = \frac{\text{Cost of goods sold}}{\text{Average inventory}}$$

- This ratio measures how quickly inventory is sold. The higher the turnover, the better the performance.

$$\text{Days in inventory} = \frac{\text{Ending inventory}}{\text{(Cost of goods sold / 365)}}$$

$$\text{Operating cycle} = \text{Days sales in accounts receivable} + \text{Days in inventory}$$

- Indicates the number of days between the acquisition of inventory and the realization of cash from selling the inventory—the "cash to cash" cycle.

$$\text{Working capital turnover} = \frac{\text{Sales (net)}}{\text{Average working capital}}$$

- This ratio indicates how effectively working capital is used.

$$\text{Asset turnover} = \frac{\text{Sales (net)}}{\text{Average total assets}}$$

- This ratio is indicative of a firm's effective use of its assets. A high ratio indicates effective asset use to generate sales.

2.3   Profitability Ratios

Measures of the success or failure of an enterprise for a given period of time.

$$\text{Net profit margin} = \frac{\text{Net income}}{\text{Net sales}}$$

$$\text{Net operating margin percentage} = \frac{\text{Net operating income}}{\text{Net sales}}$$

$$\text{Gross (profit) margin} = \frac{\text{Sales (net)} - \text{Cost of goods sold}}{\text{Sales (net)}}$$

$$\text{Return on assets} = \frac{\text{Net income}}{\text{Average total assets}}$$

2.4   Long-Term Debt-Paying Ability Ratios

Measures of security for long-term creditors/investors.

$$\text{Debt to equity} = \frac{\text{Total liabilities}}{\text{Total equity}}$$

$$\text{Total debt ratio} = \frac{\text{Total liabilities}}{\text{Total assets}}$$

These ratios indicate the degree of protection to creditors in case of insolvency. The lower these ratios, the better the company's position.

Question 2   MCQ-09069

Which of the following is *least* likely to be a reasonable explanation for an increase in accounts receivable turnover?

   1. Early payment incentives for customers.

   2. Tightening of credit policy.

   3. Implementation of more aggressive collection policies.

   4. Allowance of a new grace period for customer payments.

---

1 Types of Substantive Procedures

Substantive procedures are performed to detect material misstatements at the relevant assertion level. They are required for each material transaction class, account balance, or disclosure.

Substantive procedures include:

- Tests of details of transactions and balances.
- Analytical procedures.

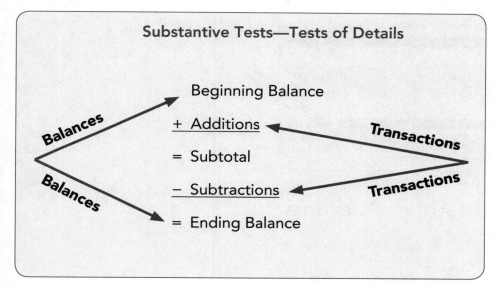

Substantive Tests—Tests of Details

Balances

Beginning Balance

+ Additions ← Transactions

= Subtotal

− Subtractions ← Transactions

Balances → = Ending Balance

2 Substantive Analytical Procedures

In certain situations, analytical procedures are a more effective and efficient means of gathering evidence than tests of details, and in those cases, analytical procedures may be used as substantive tests.

When using substantive analytical procedures, the auditor considers:

- Designing and performing substantive analytical procedures, including audit data analytics (ADAs) and any associated techniques, tools, graphics, and tables.
- Efficiency and effectiveness of analytical procedures.
- Limitations of analytical procedures.
- Documentation requirements.
- Analytical procedures used as an overall review.

3 Directional Testing

Directional testing refers to testing either forward or backward.

3.1 Tracing Forward

Tracing forward from source documents to journal entries or to the financial statements provides evidence of completeness.

3.2 Vouching Backward

Vouching backward from the financial statements or from journal entries to source documents provides evidence of existence or occurrence.

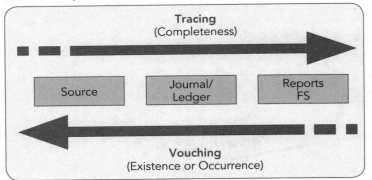

4 Common Substantive Auditing Procedures

- **F**ooting, cross-footing, and recalculation: Adding down and across; testing arithmetical accuracy of statements and schedules (valuation and allocation).

- **I**nquiry: Made of both internal and external sources.

- **V**ouching: Directional testing; looking for support for what has been recorded in the records and statements; going from the financial statement back to supporting documents (existence/occurrence).

- **E**xamination and inspection of documents/records; reading board of directors' (BOD) minutes; reviewing the financial statement (understandability and classification).

- **C**onfirmation: Direct written verification from independent third parties about account balances (existence) and transactions or events (occurrence). Also, perform **c**utoff review of year-end transactions (proper period).

- **A**nalytical procedures: Establish relationships and highlight risk areas. Also, **a**udit related accounts.

- **R**eperformance: Auditor independently performs control procedures.

- **R**econciliation: Substantiates the existence and valuation of accounts. Also, **r**ead necessary information such as meeting minutes from BOD/shareholder meetings, and obtain management **r**epresentation letter.

- **O**bservation: Provides the auditor with direct knowledge; most persuasive form of evidence in providing assurance as to the existence or occurrence of an item.

- **T**racing: Directional testing; starts with the source documents and traces forward to provide assurance that the event is being given proper recognition in the books and records (completeness; accuracy).

- **C**utoff review: The auditor should perform a cutoff review of year-end transactions, especially inventory, cash, purchases, sales, and accruals.

- **A**uditing related accounts simultaneously: Certain accounts can be audited simultaneously, including long-term liabilities and interest expense, capital additions to PP&E and repairs and maintenance expense, and investments and investment income.

- **R**epresentation letter: At the conclusion of fieldwork, the independent auditor must obtain a management representation letter from the client.

- **S**ubsequent events review: Procedures required for the period after the balance sheet date up to the date of the auditor's report.

Question 1   MCQ-08112

Which financial statement assertion is violated when an expense occurring in one year is *not* recorded until the following year?

1. Accuracy
2. Classification
3. Completeness
4. Occurrence

---

5 Interim Substantive Procedures

- Performing substantive procedures at an interim date requires additional work to extend audit conclusions to period end.

- Interim substantive procedures should only be performed when the risk of material misstatement is low.

Question 2   MCQ-09839

Which of the following is a substantive procedure?

1. Verifying that the vouchers payable package is appropriately approved.
2. Observing the payroll distribution on an unannounced basis.
3. Observing the preparation of the accounts receivable aging schedule.
4. Examining open vouchers as part of the search for unrecorded liabilities.

---

1 Auditing Accounts Receivable

1.1 Accounts Receivable Confirmations

Confirmation of accounts receivable is required unless:

- receivables are immaterial; or
- confirmation would be ineffective; or
- inherent and control risks are very low and evidence provided by other procedures sufficiently reduces audit risk.

The auditor must document the basis for omission of confirmation procedures.

1.2 Positive Confirmations

Positive confirmations should be used for large receivables. The customers are requested to return a statement to the auditor indicating that they agree with the amount. Positive confirmations should be sent for:

- Large individual accounts
- Expected errors
- Items in dispute
- Weak internal control
- Old balances

1.3 Negative Confirmations

Negative confirmations are less effective than positive confirmations. When negative confirmations are used, an answer is requested only if the amount stated is incorrect. Negative confirmations may be used when:

- inherent and control risks are low; and
- a large number of small balances are being confirmed; and
- there is no reason to expect that the recipients will ignore the confirmations.

1.4 Confirmation Nonresponses

When the auditor has not received replies to positive confirmation requests, the auditor should apply alternative procedures to the nonresponsive accounts to reduce audit risk to an acceptably low level. The nature of alternative procedures varies with the account and the assertion.

The omission of alternative procedures may be warranted when:

- the auditor has not identified unusual qualitative factors or systematic characteristics related to the nonresponses; and
- treating the aggregate nonresponses as 100 percent misstatements would not affect the auditor's conclusion about whether the financial statements are materially misstated.

1.5 Accounts Receivable Confirmation Exceptions

Confirmation exceptions occur when there is a disparity between the amount of the receivable recorded in the client's accounting records and the amount of the receivable confirmed by the client's customer. For confirmation exceptions, the auditor should determine whether the exception is due to a timing difference or a misstatement.

1.6 Evaluating Results

- The auditor should evaluate the evidence provided by confirmations and alternative procedures to determine whether sufficient evidence has been obtained about all the applicable financial statement assertions.
- If the evidence gathered is not sufficient, the auditor should request additional confirmations or extend other tests.

Question 1   MCQ-09833

After multiple attempts, an auditor is unable to obtain a response for several positive requests for year-end accounts receivable confirmations. An appropriate alternative procedure to verify the existence of accounts receivable is:

1. Visit the customer selected for confirmation and review documents in their possession.
2. Obtain the aging of accounts receivable and trace it to the general ledger control account.
3. Examine the applicable sales order, shipping document, and subsequent cash receipts.
4. Examine subsequent cash disbursements and related receiving reports.

---

2 Auditing Cash

2.1 Bank Confirmations

Bank confirmations should be sent to all banks with whom the entity has done business. Bank transfer schedules, bank reconciliations, and cutoff bank statements should also be used.

2.2 Fraudulent Cash Schemes

The auditor should look for fraudulent cash schemes during the audit.

2.2.1 Kiting

- Kiting occurs when a check drawn on one bank is deposited in another bank and no record is made of the first disbursement.

- To detect kiting, cash deposits at the end of a period and paid checks returned with the bank statements of the next period should be examined (bank transfer schedule). Check dates will indicate whether the receiving bank recorded the receipt before the recorded disbursement date.

2.2.2 Lapping

- Lapping occurs when current receipts of cash/checks are withheld (i.e., stolen) and not recorded. Subsequent receipts are applied to the prior accounts.

- Safeguard—Use a lockbox system.

- To detect lapping, use the deposit slip test—trace deposit items from the deposit slip to posting in the customer account.

Question 2 — MCQ-09835

At KRM Corporation, an employee performed the following scheme:

Customer	*Employee*
Andrew Vent came in with $100 cash to pay off his outstanding receivable.	The employee stole the $100 cash.
Bob Butterfield paid off $100 of his outstanding receivable.	The employee credited Andrew Kent's account for $100.
Chris Copper paid off $200 of his outstanding receivable.	The employee credited Bob Butterfield's account for $100 and stole the remainder $100.

What best describes this scheme?

1. Kiting
2. Lapping
3. Identity theft
4. Fraudulent financial reporting

1 Auditing Revenue

1.1 Flowchart—Cash Receipts and Accounts Receivable

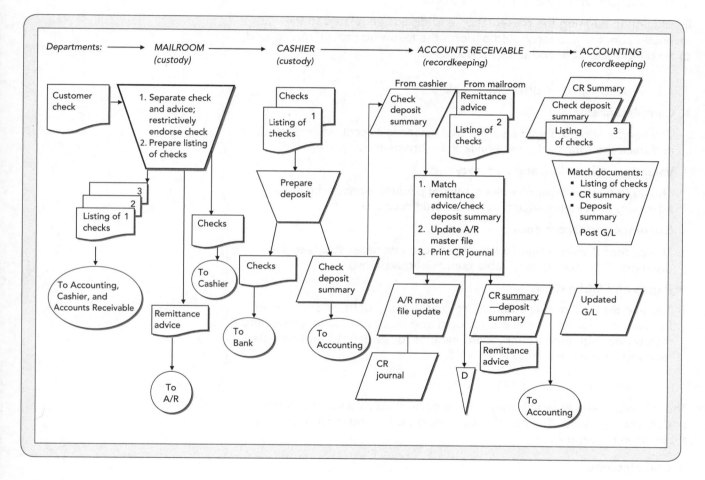

1.2 Segregation of Duties

- **Authorization:** Sales order and credit
- **Record Keeping:** Billing/accounts receivable/accounting
- **Custody:** Warehouse and shipping

1.3 Risk of Overstatement

Management may be pressured to overstate revenues to meet EPS targets and improve balance sheet ratios. For these reasons, management may:

- Record fictitious sales (existence assertion).
- Hold open the sales journal into next year (cutoff).
- Ship goods not ordered, which will be returned next year (improper revenue recognition).

1.4 Substantive Procedures

In addition to auditing the presentation and disclosure related to the revenue cycle, the auditor should perform the following procedures related to accounts receivable and sales transactions.

1.4.1 Auditing Accounts Receivable

- **Completeness**

   The auditor should obtain an aged trial balance of accounts receivable and trace the total to the general ledger control account.

- **Valuation, Allocation, and Accuracy**

   The auditor should examine the results of confirmations and test the adequacy of the allowance for uncollectible accounts.

- **Existence and Occurrence**

   The auditor should confirm a sample of accounts receivable (see the discussion of accounts receivable confirmations below).

- **Rights and Obligations**

   The auditor should review bank confirmations and debt agreements for liens on receivables. The auditor should also inquire of management and review debt agreements and board minutes for evidence that accounts receivable have been factored or sold.

1.4.2 Auditing Sales Transactions

The following tests of details may also be performed as tests of controls or dual-purpose tests. The cutoff procedure is performed most often as a substantive procedure.

- **Completeness**

   The auditor should trace a sample of shipping documents to the corresponding sales invoices and to the sales journal and accounts receivable subsidiary ledger.

- **Cutoff**

   The auditor should compare a sample of sales invoices from shortly before and after year-end with the shipment dates and with the dates the sales were recorded in the sales journal. The auditor should also analyze the record of sales returns after year-end.

■ Valuation, Allocation, and Accuracy

The auditor should compare prices and terms on a sample of sales invoices with authorized price lists and terms of trade to determine whether sales are recorded at the appropriate amount.

■ Existence and Occurrence

The auditor should vouch a sample of sales transactions from the sales journal to the sales invoice back to the customer order and shipping documents.

■ Understandability and Classification

The auditor should examine a sample of sales invoices for proper classification into the appropriate revenue accounts.

Question 1   MCQ-01625

Which of the following controls most likely would assure that all billed sales are correctly posted to the accounts receivable ledger?

1. Daily sales summaries are compared to daily postings to the accounts receivable ledger.

2. Each sales invoice is supported by a prenumbered shipping document.

3. The accounts receivable ledger is reconciled daily to the control account in the general ledger.

4. Each shipment on credit is supported by a prenumbered sales invoice.

Question 2   MCQ-09847

Tracing shipping documents to sales invoices provides evidence that:

1. Sales billed to customers were actually shipped.

2. Shipments to customers were properly invoiced.

3. Shipments to customers were recorded as sales.

4. All goods ordered by customers were shipped.

---

2 Auditing Expenditures

2.1 Segregation of Duties

- **Purchasing Department:** Approve and prepare purchase order.
- **Receiving Department:** Receive goods, match with purchase order (blind copy), and prepare receiving reports.
- **Vouchers Payable Department:** Match documents, purchase order, receiving reports, invoice; prepare and approve voucher, verify accuracy.
- **Treasury Department:** Review documents, prepare check & remittance advice, sign checks, cancel voucher package.

2.2 Substantive Procedures

In addition to auditing the presentation and disclosure related to the expenditure cycle, the auditor should perform the following procedures related to accounts payable and purchase transactions.

2.2.1 Auditing Accounts Payable

- **Completeness**

  The auditor should perform a search for unrecorded liabilities.

- **Valuation, Allocation, and Accuracy**

  The auditor should obtain the accounts payable listing, foot the listing, and agree the listing to the general ledger, obtain a sample of vendor statements and agree the amounts to the vendor accounts, and review the results of any accounts payable confirmations.

- **Existence and Occurrence**

  The auditor should vouch selected amounts from the accounts payable listing to the voucher packages. The auditor may also confirm accounts payable. Accounts payable confirmations are not required because good external evidence to support accounts payable is generally available. However, confirmations of accounts payable may be sent when internal control is weak, when there are disputed amounts, or when monthly vendor statements are not available. Typically, vendors with small or zero balances would be selected for confirmation.

- **Rights and Obligations**

  The auditor should review a sample of voucher packages for the presence of the purchase requisition, purchase order, receiving report and vendor invoice to verify that the accounts payable are owed by the entity.

2.2.2 Auditing Purchase Transactions

The following substantive tests may also be performed as tests of controls or dual-purpose tests.

■ **Completeness**

The auditor should trace a sample of vouchers to the purchase journal.

■ **Cutoff**

The auditor should compare dates on a sample of vouchers with the dates the transactions were recorded in the purchase journal. The auditor should also examine purchases before and after year-end to determine if they were recorded in the proper period.

■ **Valuation, Allocation, and Accuracy**

The auditor should recompute the mathematical accuracy of a sample of vendor invoices.

■ **Existence and Occurrence**

The auditor should test a sample of vouchers for authorization and the presence of the receiving report.

■ **Understandability and Classification**

The auditor should verify the account classification of a sample of purchases.

Question 3   MCQ-09849

An auditor searching for unrecorded payables most likely would:

1. Obtain a sample of vendor invoices and recalculate the invoice amount.

2. Obtain the accounts payable listing and agree to subsequent cash payments.

3. Compare cash disbursements made prior to year-end with vendor invoices.

4. Compare subsequent bank statements with the accounts payable listing.

---

3 Auditing PP&E

The property, plant, and equipment cycle includes all tangible long-term asset functions (e.g., purchasing, maintenance and repair, depreciation, retirement).

- **Purchases and Retirements:** Verify that proper authorization was obtained, and that proper procedures were followed. The auditor should vouch additions to fixed assets by examining documentation and inspecting the actual asset (existence). The auditor should also select older fixed assets from the subsidiary ledger and try to locate the assets as a means of testing for unrecorded retirements (existence). The auditor should review related repair and maintenance accounts for any improper classification of additions and repairs as expenses (completeness and classification).

- **Authorization:** Verify Board approval of substantial purchases.

- **Physical Security:** Serially numbered plates should be on assets; the control account should include all appropriate information.

- **Depreciation:** Verify that written policies and records are maintained; recalculate expense and ensure conformity with GAAP (valuation and accuracy).

- **Impairments:** Check for adjustments for impairments (valuation and accuracy).

Question 4   MCQ-08325

An auditor analyzes repair and maintenance accounts primarily to obtain evidence in support of the audit assertion that all:

   1. Noncapitalizable expenditures for repairs and maintenance have been recorded in the proper period.

   2. Expenditures for property and equipment have been recorded in the proper period.

   3. Noncapitalizable expenditures for repairs and maintenance have been properly charged to expense.

   4. Expenditures for property and equipment have not been charged to expense.

---

4 Auditing Payroll

4.1 Segregation of Duties

Controls including proper segregation of duties are essential to prevent common problems in the payroll and personnel cycle—fictitious employees and falsification of hours.

4.1.1 Authorization

- **Authorization to Employ and Pay:** The human resource department's function is to hire new employees and maintain personnel records (hire date, salary, and position).
- **Supervision:** All pay base data (hours, absences, and time off) should be approved by an employee's immediate supervisor.

4.1.2 Record Keeping

- **Timekeeping and Cost Accounting:** Data on which pay is based should be accumulated independent of any other function. Hourly employees should use time clocks. Supervisors should compare job time tickets to signed employee clock cards.
- **Payroll Check Preparation:** The payroll department computes salary based on information received. This department is responsible for issuing the unsigned payroll checks.

4.1.3 Custody of Assets

The treasurer is responsible for signing the payroll checks.

4.1.4 Auditing Payroll and Personnel

- The auditor reviews the payroll account to determine that only authorized people are being paid, and that they are receiving the right amounts. The auditor should verify time records, and perform recalculations of payroll amounts and any year-end accruals (valuation assertion).
- A person who has no other payroll function should distribute the payroll checks. This person is often referred to as the paymaster. Employees should be required to show ID before receiving paychecks.

4.2 Substantive Procedures

When internal control over payroll is effective, the auditor generally focuses substantive procedures on the valuation and accuracy assertion. The following audit procedures should be performed to verify the accuracy of payroll amounts:

- Vouch time on payroll summaries by selecting a payroll register entry and comparing to time cards and approved time reports.
- Compare total recorded payroll with total payroll checks issued.

- Test extensions and footings of payroll.
- Verify pay rates and payroll deductions with employee records from personnel.
- Recalculate gross and net pay on a test basis.
- Recalculate any year-end accruals.
- Compare payroll costs with standards or budgets.

Substantive tests should be extended if unusual fluctuations or significant errors are noted.

Question 5   MCQ-08124

In auditing the payroll function of a client, an auditor would least likely:

1. Request specific management representations related to payroll.

2. Verify proper segregation of duties.

3. Recalculate year-end payroll accruals.

4. Apply analytical procedures.

---

5 Auditing Liabilities

When auditing debt, the auditor reviews board minutes for evidence of new debt, obtains new debt agreements, and traces new debt to the financial statements (completeness), recomputes gains and losses, interest expense and interest payable (valuation and accuracy), and verifies proper presentation and disclosure.

6 Auditing Owners' Equity and Treasury Stock

The audit of owners' equity and treasury stock includes examining transactions related to the sale and repurchase of stock, related payments, dividends, and retained earnings.

6.1 Substantive Procedures

- **Treasury Stock:** Examine and reconcile the number of shares in the treasury stock account, and trace all transactions to the accounting records and the board minutes (existence and completeness).

- **Stock Transactions:** Vouch all transactions to supporting documentation (existence).

- **Minutes of Board Meetings:** Verify that all stock issuances, dividends declared, and treasury stock transactions have been authorized by the board.

- **Articles of Incorporation:** Read the articles and prepare excerpts for the permanent file.

- **Stock Transfer Agents:** Use third-party confirmations to provide evidence of shares authorized, issued, and outstanding (completeness and existence).

- **Stock Certificate Book:** If there is no transfer agent, review the stock certificate book to provide evidence of proper stock transaction accounting (completeness and existence).

- **Retained Earnings:** Analyze retained earnings account since inception (or since the last audit) and review the propriety of any direct entries to retained earnings (valuation), and determine whether any appropriations are necessary (understandability and classification).

Question 6   MCQ-08868

An audit program for the examination of the retained earnings account should include a step that requires verification of the:

1. Market value used to charge retained earnings to account for a two-for-one stock split.

2. Approval of the adjustment to the beginning balance as a result of a write-down of an account receivable.

3. Authorization for both cash and stock dividends.

4. Gain or loss resulting from disposition of treasury shares.

Auditing Final Review

1 Auditing Inventory

- **Controls:** Good controls should exist between purchasing, receiving, storage, and shipping.

- **Observation:** Observation of the physical inventory count is required, although failure to observe can be mitigated by alternative procedures. Observation and test counts provide evidence related to existence and completeness.

- **Calculation:** The auditor should test the physical inventory report by tracing test counts and verifying mathematical accuracy.

- **Consigned Goods:** The auditor should ascertain that consigned inventory on hand is excluded from the physical count, while goods out on consignment are included in inventory.

- **Related Accounts:** Simultaneous procedures should be undertaken for accounts related to inventory (purchases, sales, returns, and allowances).

- **Quantity:** Cutoff procedures should be performed for purchases and sales.

- **Presentation:** GAAP should be followed.

- **Analytical Review:** Overall reasonableness of amounts and disclosures should be evaluated; ratio analysis may be used.

- **Obsolete or Damaged Goods:** The inventory listing should be reviewed for slow-moving items; inquiries should be made regarding obsolete or damaged goods.

Question 1　　　　　　　　　　　　　　　MCQ-09830

In auditing a manufacturing entity, which of the following procedures would an auditor most likely perform to determine whether slow-moving, defective, and obsolete items included in inventory are properly identified?

1. Test the mathematical accuracy of the inventory report.

2. Inquire of management about whether inventory has been pledged or assigned.

3. Tour the manufacturing plant or production facility.

4. Test the computation of standard overhead rates.

---

2 Auditing Investments

The auditor must ensure that GAAP is consistently applied, gains and losses are accurately computed and disclosed, investment income is properly reported, valuation is fairly stated and disclosed, and the investments in fact exist and are owned by the entity under audit.

- **Segregation of Duties:** Authorization (usually the board of directors), the custodial function, and record keeping should be segregated.
- **Confirmation From Third Parties:** This should be obtained if investments are held by an independent, third-party custodian.
- **Physical Inspection:** For securities on hand, a physical inspection should be performed.
- **Cutoff Procedures:** These procedures should be applied to purchases, sales, and investment income.
- **Conformance With GAAP:** Derivative, fair value through net income method/equity method, trading, available-for-sale, and held-to-maturity classifications should be used.
- **Computations:** Gains, losses, discount or premium amortization, and interest or dividend income should be independently calculated.
- **Management Representations:** The auditor should inquire of management and obtain written representation concerning management's intent and ability to hold or to exercise significant influence over investments.
- **Reasonableness and Appropriateness:** These factors should be evaluated as they relate to assumptions, market variables, valuation models, and any decline in fair value.
- **Special Skill or Knowledge:** The auditor may need special skill or knowledge to plan and perform auditing procedures for certain assertions about derivatives and securities.

Question 2 MCQ-08905

Which of the following provides the best evidence supporting the existence of marketable securities included in the client's financial statements?

1. A custodial statement received and held by the client.
2. The client's securities ledger.
3. Broker's advice regarding purchases and sales of marketable securities.
4. A year-end listing of market prices for the securities obtained by reference to the Wall Street Journal.

1 Overview

When audit procedures indicate that there are actual or potential litigation, claims, or assessments, the auditor should seek direct communication with the entity's external legal counsel through a letter of inquiry regarding litigation, claims and assessments.

■ The auditor should inquire about specific litigation (if identified), including the timing and the degree of probability of an unfavorable outcome.

■ The lawyer's response is sent directly to the auditor.

■ No response or a refusal to cooperate is considered a scope limitation.

Question 1   MCQ-09851

Which limitation on response from an attorney in response to auditor's inquiry may result in a qualified opinion?

1. The client's refusal to permit inquiry of the attorney.

2. The attorney's refusal to respond when the attorney has given substantial attention to the matter.

3. An inherent uncertainty making it difficult for a lawyer to form conclusions regarding pending litigation.

4. The attorney limits replies to matters to which he or she has given substantial attention.

Question 2   MCQ-09047

Which of the following best describes the purpose of an auditor's external inquiry sent to the client's attorney?

1. To develop an appropriate understanding of controls in place with respect to the recognition of litigation, claims, and assessments.

2. To evaluate the operating effectiveness of controls in place with respect to the recognition of litigation, claims, and assessments.

3. To corroborate information provided by management with respect to litigation, claims, and assessments.

4. To obtain reasonable assurance from the client's attorney regarding fair presentation of litigation, claims, and assessments in the financial statements.

---

2 Sample Attorney Letter

[Company Letterhead]

[Appropriate Addressee]:

In connection with an audit of our financial statements at (balance sheet date) and for the (period) then ended, management of the Company has prepared, and furnished to our auditors (name and address of auditors), a description and evaluation of certain contingencies, including those set forth below involving matters with respect to which you have been engaged and to which you have devoted substantive attention on behalf of the Company in the form of legal consultation or representation. These contingencies are regarded by management of the Company as material for this purpose (management may indicate a materiality limit if an understanding has been reached with the auditor). Your response should include matters that existed at (balance sheet date) and during the period from that date to the date of your response.

Pending or Threatened Litigation

[Ordinarily management's information would include (i) the nature of the litigation, (ii) the progress of the case to date, (iii) how management is responding or intends to respond to the litigation, and (iv) an evaluation of the likelihood of an unfavorable outcome and an estimate, if one can be made, of the amount or range of potential loss.]

This letter will serve as our consent for you to furnish to our auditor all the information requested therein. Accordingly, please furnish to our auditors such explanation, if any, that you consider necessary to supplement the foregoing information, including an explanation of those matters as to which your views may differ from those stated and an identification of the omission of any pending or threatened litigation, claims, and assessments or a statement that the list of such matters is complete.

Unasserted Claims and Assessments

[Ordinarily management's information would include (i) the nature of the matter, (ii) how management intends to respond if the claim is asserted, and (iii) an evaluation of the likelihood of an unfavorable outcome and an estimate, if one can be made, of the amount or range of potential loss.]

Please furnish to our auditors such explanation, if any, that you consider necessary to supplement the foregoing information, including an explanation of those matters as to which your views may differ from those stated.

We understand that whenever, in the course of performing legal services for us with respect to a matter recognized to involve an unasserted possible claim or assessment that may call for financial statement disclosure, if you have formed a professional conclusion that we should disclose or consider disclosure concerning such possible claim or assessment, as a matter of professional responsibility to us, you will so advise us and will consult with us concerning the question of such disclosure and the applicable requirements of Financial Accounting Standards Board (FASB) Accounting Standards Codification (ASC) 450, Contingencies. Please specifically confirm to our auditors that our understanding is correct.

Please specifically identify the nature of and reasons for any limitations on your response.

Very truly yours,

[Name]

1 Auditor Responsibility

The auditor is responsible for evaluating audit evidence to determine whether there is *"substantial doubt"* that the client will be able to continue as a going concern for a reasonable period of time, as defined by the financial reporting framework used (FASB—one year after financial statements are issued or available to be issued; GASB—one year beyond the date of the financial statements).

2 Emphasis-of-Matter or Explanatory Paragraph

If substantial doubt exists, an *emphasis-of-matter paragraph* (nonissuer) or explanatory paragraph (issuer) stating the auditor's concerns should be added to the auditor's opinion. The words *"substantial doubt"* and *"going concern"* must be included.

Emphasis of Matter

The accompanying financial statements have been prepared assuming that the Company will continue as a going concern. As discussed in Note X to the financial statements, the Company has suffered recurring losses from operations and has a net capital deficiency, and has stated that substantial doubt exists about the Company's ability to continue as a going concern. Management's evaluation of the events and conditions and management's plans regarding these matters are also described in Note X. The financial statements do not include any adjustments that might result from the outcome of this uncertainty. Our opinion is not modified with respect to this matter.

Question 1   MCQ-08819

Calibro, CPA, believes that there is substantial doubt about the ability of Canto Company, a nonissuer, to continue as a going concern. This matter is appropriately disclosed in Canto's financial statements. Calibro should:

1. Issue an unmodified opinion with an other-matter paragraph describing the situation.

2. Issue a qualified opinion due to the fact that there is substantial doubt about the ability of Canto Company to continue as a going concern.

3. Issue an unmodified opinion with an emphasis-of-matter paragraph describing the situation.

4. Withdraw from the engagement, to minimize the association with financial statements that may be misleading.

3 Audit Approach

3.1 Audit Procedures

The following audit procedures (ADMITS) may indicate that there is a problem with the entity's ability to continue as a going concern:

- **A**nalytical procedures
- Review of compliance with terms of **d**ebt/loan agreements
- Review of the **m**inutes of stockholder/board meetings
- **I**nquiry of client's legal counsel
- Confirmation of the details of financial support arrangements with **t**hird parties
- Review of **s**ubsequent events

3.2 Conditions

Conditions (FINE) that may indicate a problem include:

- **F**inancial difficulties
- **I**nternal matters (e.g., work stoppages, labor difficulties)
- **N**egative financial trends
- **E**xternal matters (e.g., legal proceedings, new legislation)

3.3 Mitigating Factors

The auditor should consider *mitigating factors*. Both intent and ability are required.

3.4 Subsequent Periods

If doubt is removed in a subsequent period, the going concern paragraph need not be repeated.

Question 2   MCQ-08128

Davis, CPA, believes there is substantial doubt about the ability of Hill Co. to continue as a going concern for a reasonable period of time. In evaluating Hill's plans for dealing with the adverse effects of future conditions and events, Davis most likely would consider, as a mitigating factor, Hill's plans to:

1. Accelerate research and development projects related to future products.
2. Accumulate treasury stock at prices favorable to Hill's historic price range.
3. Purchase equipment and production facilities currently being leased.
4. Negotiate reductions in required dividends being paid on preferred stock.

Control Deficiency

A control deficiency exists when the design or operation of a control does not allow management or employees, in the normal course of their assigned functions, **to prevent, or detect and correct** [*prevent and detect*], misstatements on a timely basis.

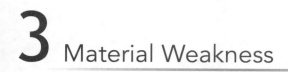

Significant Deficiency

A significant deficiency is a deficiency (or a combination of deficiencies) in internal control [*over financial reporting*] that is less severe than a material weakness, yet important enough to merit attention by **those charged with governance** [*responsible for oversight of the company's financial reporting*].

> 📌 **Note**
>
> Wording for nonissuers is shown in **bold**; wording for issuers is shown in [*brackets*].

3 Material Weakness

A material weakness is a deficiency (or a combination of deficiencies) in internal control [*over financial reporting*] such that there is a reasonable possibility that a material misstatement of the **entity's** [*company's annual or interim*] financial statements will not be **prevented, or detected and corrected,** [*prevented or detected*] on a timely basis.

3.1 Reasonable Possibility

"Reasonable possibility" implies that the likelihood of an event is either reasonably possible or probable.

3.2   Indicators of Material Weakness

The following situations are indicators of material weakness in internal control:

- Identification of any level of fraud (even immaterial fraud) perpetrated by senior management.

- Restatement of previously issued financial statements to correct a material misstatement.

- Identification by the auditor of a material misstatement that would not have been detected by the entity's internal control.

- Ineffective oversight by those charged with governance.

Question 1   MCQ-09707

Significant deficiencies are control deficiencies that come to an auditor's attention that are:

1. Disclosures of information that significantly contradict the auditor's going concern assumption.

2. Material fraud or illegal acts perpetrated by high-level management.

3. Important enough to merit attention by those charged with governance.

4. Manipulation or falsification of accounting records or documents from which financial statements are prepared.

---

1 Overview

At the conclusion of fieldwork, the auditor must obtain a letter (signed by the CEO and CFO), dated as of the date of the auditor's report.

1.1 Purpose

The purposes of the representation letter are:

- to ensure that management accepts its responsibility for the assertions in the entity's financial statements; and
- to document the client's representations and responses to inquiries concerning various aspects of the audit.

1.2 Timing

The representation letter is the final piece of audit evidence. When reporting on comparative financial statements, it should address all periods covered by the report. This letter is mandatory; omission of this letter constitutes a scope limitation.

Question 1   MCQ-09834

According to U.S. GAAS, the date of the management representation letter should be:

1. As near as possible to, but not after, the date of the auditor's report.
2. The same as the date of the auditor's report.
3. As near as possible to, but not after, the date of the financial statements.
4. The same as the date of the financial statements.

---

2 Sample Representation Letter

Management Representation Letter

[Entity Letterhead]

To *[Auditor]*   *[Date]*

This letter is provided in connection with your audit of the financial statements of ABC Company, which comprise the balance sheet as of December 31, 20XX, and the related statements of income, changes in stockholders' equity, and cash flows for the year then ended, and the related notes to the financial statements, for the purpose of expressing an opinion on whether the financial statements are presented fairly, in all material respects, in accordance with accounting principles generally accepted in the United States (U.S. GAAP).

Certain representations in this letter are described as being limited to matters that are material. Items are considered material, regardless of size, if they involve an omission or misstatement of accounting information that, in the light of surrounding circumstances, makes it probable that the judgment of a reasonable person relying on the information would be changed or influenced by the omission or misstatement.

Except where otherwise stated below, immaterial matters less than $*[insert amount]* collectively are not considered to be exceptions that require disclosure for the purpose of the following representations. This amount is not necessarily indicative of amounts that would require adjustment to or disclosure in the financial statements.

We confirm that, [*to the best of our knowledge and belief, having made such inquiries as we considered necessary for the purpose of appropriately informing ourselves*] [*as of (date of auditor's report)*]:

Financial Statements

1. We have fulfilled our responsibilities, as set out in the terms of the audit engagement dated [*insert date*], for the preparation and fair presentation of the financial statements in accordance with U.S. GAAP.

2. We acknowledge our responsibility for the design, implementation, and maintenance of internal control relevant to the preparation and fair presentation of financial statements that are free from material misstatement, whether due to fraud or error.

3. We acknowledge our responsibility for the design, implementation, and maintenance of internal control to prevent and detect fraud.

4. Significant assumptions used by us in making accounting estimates, including those measured at fair value, are reasonable.

5. Related party relationships and transactions have been appropriately accounted for and disclosed in accordance with the requirements of U.S. GAAP.

6. All events subsequent to the date of the financial statements and for which U.S. GAAP requires adjustment or disclosure have been adjusted or disclosed.

7. The effects of uncorrected misstatements are immaterial, both individually and in the aggregate, to the financial statements as a whole. A list of the uncorrected misstatements is attached to the representation letter.

8. The effects of all known or possible litigation and claims have been accounted for and disclosed in accordance with U.S. GAAP.

[*Any other matters that the auditor may consider appropriate.*]

(continued)

(continued)

Information Provided

9. We have provided you with:

   a. Access to all information, of which we are aware that is relevant to the preparation and fair presentation of the financial statements such as records, documentation and other matters;

   b. Additional information that you have requested from us for the purpose of the audit; and

   c. Unrestricted access to persons within the entity from whom you determined it necessary to obtain audit evidence.

10. All transactions have been recorded in the accounting records and are reflected in the financial statements.

11. We have disclosed to you the results of our assessment of the risk that the financial statements may be materially misstated as a result of fraud.

12. We have [*no knowledge of any*] [*disclosed to you all information that we are aware of regarding*] fraud or suspected fraud affecting the entity and involves:

   a. Management,

   b. Employees who have significant roles in internal control, or

   c. Others where the fraud could have a material effect on the financial statements.

13. We have [*no knowledge of any*] [*disclosed to you all information that we are aware of regarding*] allegations of fraud, or suspected fraud, affecting the entity's financial statements communicated by employees, former employees, analysts, regulators, or others.

14. We disclosed to you all known instances of noncompliance or suspected noncompliance with laws and regulations whose effects should be considered when preparing financial statements.

15. We [*have disclosed to you all known actual or possible*][*are not aware of any pending or threatened*] litigation and claims whose effects should be considered when preparing financial statements [*and we have not consulted legal counsel concerning litigation or claims*].

16. We have disclosed to you the identity of the entity's related parties and all the related party relationships and transactions of which we are aware.

[*Any other matters that the auditor may consider necessary.*]

_____

[*Name of Chief Executive Officer and Title*]

_____

[*Name of Chief Financial Officer and Title*]

1 Types of Subsequent Events

A subsequent event occurs between the balance sheet date and the date the financial statements are issued. Subsequent events may require either adjustment to the financial statements or additional disclosure. Subsequent events are divided into two categories.

1.1 Recognized Events

Recognized events are conditions existing on or before the balance sheet date. Recognized events usually require adjustment to the financial statements.

1.2 Nonrecognized Events

Nonrecognized events are conditions existing after the balance sheet date. Nonrecognized events usually require disclosure, but no financial statement adjustment.

Question 1   MCQ-08118

A client acquired 25% of its outstanding capital stock after year-end but prior to the date of the auditor's report. The auditor should:

1. Advise management to adjust the balance sheet to reflect the acquisition.

2. Issue pro forma financial statements giving effect to the acquisition as if it had occurred at year-end.

3. Advise management to disclose the acquisition in the notes to the financial statements.

4. Disclose the acquisition in the opinion paragraph of the auditor's report.

2 Auditor's Responsibility

The auditor has an active responsibility to investigate subsequent events during the period from the balance sheet date to the date of the auditor's report. Responsibilities include:

- Reviewing **p**ost balance sheet transactions.
- Obtaining a **r**epresentation letter from management.
- **I**nquiry
- Reading the **m**inutes of stockholder, director, and other committee meetings.
- **E**xamining the latest available interim statements.

3 Responsibility After the Auditor's Report Date

The auditor has no active responsibility after the date of the auditor's report, but cannot ignore information coming to his/her attention. If subsequent events result in adjustments or disclosures that are made after the original date of the auditor's report, the auditor may dual date the report to extend responsibility only for the particular subsequent event.

Question 2   MCQ-09050

An auditor issues a report dated 2/12/Year 2 on financial statements for the year ended 12/31/Year 1. Which best describes the auditor's responsibility for an event occurring on 2/1/Year 2 and an event occurring on 3/1/Year 2?

1. The auditor has an active responsibility to investigate both events.

2. The auditor has an active responsibility to investigate the 2/1/Year 2 event, but no responsibility concerning the 3/1/Year 2 event.

3. The auditor has an active responsibility to investigate the 2/1/Year 2 event, and must also consider the effect of the 3/1/Year 2 event if it comes to his/her attention.

4. The auditor has no responsibility for either event, since both occur after the date of the financial statements.

---

1 Auditor Action

If the auditor becomes aware of material information after the report's issuance and knows persons are currently relying or likely to rely on the financial statements, the auditor should advise the client to immediately disclose the information and its impact on the financial statements. If the financial impact cannot be timely ascertained, notification should be made that the financial statements cannot be relied upon.

2 Client Refuses to Follow Procedures

The auditor must be satisfied with the client's action; if not, the auditor should notify the board of directors and the client that the audit report cannot be associated with the financial statements. The auditor should also notify any regulatory agencies and any persons known to be relying on the statements and report.

Question 1   MCQ-09775

Which of the following events occurring after the issuance of the auditor's report most likely would cause the auditor to make further inquiries about the previously issued financial statements?

1. The company issues a bond for a material amount.

2. Loss of a plant as the result of a fire.

3. Purchase of a business that has revenues equivalent to the entity.

4. The discovery of information regarding a material unrecorded expense that occurred during the year under audit.

IV Forming Conclusions and Reporting

1 Opinion Types

1.1 Unmodified (Unqualified) Opinion

An unmodified opinion states that the financial statements present fairly, in all material respects, the financial position, results of operations, and cash flows of the entity, in conformity with the applicable financial reporting framework.

1.1.1 Emphasis-of-Matter, Other-Matter, Explanatory, and Critical Audit Matters Paragraphs

These are additional communications added to the auditor's report without modifying the auditor's opinion.

1.2 Modified Opinions

The auditor's report is modified when the auditor concludes that the financial statements as a whole are materially misstated (GAAP issue) or when the auditor is unable to obtain sufficient appropriate audit evidence to conclude that the financial statements as a whole are free from material misstatement (GAAS issue).

1.2.1 Qualified Opinion

A qualified opinion states that *except for* the effects of the matter(s) to which the qualification relates, "the financial statements present fairly. . ." It is used for GAAS or GAAP issues.

1.2.2 Adverse Opinion

An adverse opinion states that the financial statements do not present fairly. It is used for GAAP issues.

1.2.3 Disclaimer of Opinion

A disclaimer of opinion states that auditor does not express an opinion on the financial statements. It is used for GAAS issues.

2 Unmodified Opinion (Nonissuer)

Financial statements are presented fairly in all material respects. The following is an unmodified option for a nonissuer reporting on a single year.

Independent Auditor's Report

[*Appropriate Addressee*]

Report on the Financial Statements[1]

We have audited the accompanying financial statements of ABC Company, which comprise the balance sheet as of December 31, 20X1, and the related statements of income, changes in stockholders' equity, and cash flows for the year then ended, and the related notes to the financial statements.

Management's Responsibility for the Financial Statement

Management is responsible for the preparation and fair presentation of these financial statements in accordance with accounting principles generally accepted in the United States of America; this includes the design, implementation, and maintenance of internal control relevant to the preparation and fair presentation of financial statements that are free from material misstatement whether due to fraud or error.

Auditor's Responsibility

Our responsibility is to express an opinion on these financial statements based on our audit. We conducted our audit in accordance with auditing standards generally accepted in the United States of America. Those standards require that we plan and perform the audit to obtain reasonable assurance about whether the financial statements are free from material misstatement.

An audit involves performing procedures to obtain audit evidence about the amounts and disclosures in the financial statements. The procedures selected depend on the auditor's judgment, including the assessment of the risks of material misstatement of the financial statements, whether due to fraud or error. In making those risk assessments, the auditor considers internal control relevant to the entity's preparation and fair presentation of the financial statements in order to design audit procedures that are appropriate in the circumstances, but not for the purpose of expressing an opinion on the effectiveness of the entity's internal control. Accordingly, we express no such opinion. An audit also includes evaluating the appropriateness of accounting policies used and the reasonableness of significant accounting estimates made by management, as well as evaluating the overall presentation of the financial statements.

We believe that the audit evidence we have obtained is sufficient and appropriate to provide a basis for our audit opinion.

Opinion

In our opinion, the financial statements referred to above present fairly, in all material respects, the financial position of ABC Company as of December 31, 20X1, and the results of its operations and its cash flows for the year then ended in accordance with accounting principles generally accepted in the United States of America.

Report on Other Legal and Regulatory Requirements

[*Form and content of this section of the auditor's report will vary depending on the nature of the auditor's other reporting responsibilities.*]

[*Auditor's signature*]
[*Auditor's city and state*]
[*Date of the auditor's report*]

[1] "Report on the Financial Statements" is unnecessary in circumstances when the second subtitle, "Report on Legal and Regulatory Requirements," is not used.

---

3 Audits of Group Financial Statements

When an auditor acts as the auditor of group financial statements, the auditor must determine whether to make reference to any component auditors in the auditor's report on the group financial statements.

3.1 Making Reference to the Component Auditor

When making reference to the component auditor, the auditor's report on the group financial statements should clearly indicate that the component was audited by the component auditor and should include the magnitude of the portion of the financial statements audited by the component auditor.

3.1.1 U.S. GAAS

Under U.S. GAAS, the name of the component auditor may be included in the auditor's report only if permission is granted by the component auditor and the component auditor's report is presented with the auditor's report on the group financial statements.

3.1.2 Auditor's Report Referencing the Audit of a Component Auditor (Nonissuer)

Independent Auditor's Report

[*Appropriate Addressee*]

We have audited the accompanying consolidated financial statements of ABC Company and its subsidiaries, which comprise the consolidated balance sheets as of December 31, 20X1 and 20X0, and the related consolidated statements of income, changes in stockholders' equity, and cash flows for the year then ended, and the related notes to the financial statements.

Management's Responsibility for the Financial Statements

Management is responsible for the preparation and fair presentation of these consolidated financial statements in accordance with accounting principles generally accepted in the United States of America; this includes the design, implementation, and maintenance of internal control relevant to the preparation and fair presentation of consolidated financial statements that are free from material misstatement whether due to fraud or error.

Auditor's Responsibility

Our responsibility is to express an opinion on these consolidated financial statements based on our audits. We did not audit the financial statements of B Company, a wholly-owned subsidiary, which statements reflect total assets constituting 20 percent and 22 percent, respectively, of consolidated total assets at December 31, 20X1 and 20X0, and total revenues constituting 18 percent and 20 percent, respectively, of consolidated total revenues for the years then ended. Those statements were audited by other auditors, whose report has been furnished to us, and our opinion, insofar as it relates to the amounts included for B Company, is based solely on the report of the other auditors. We conducted our audit in accordance with auditing standards generally accepted in the United States of America. Those standards require that we plan and perform the audit to obtain reasonable assurance about whether the financial statements are free from material misstatement.

An audit involves performing procedures to obtain audit evidence about the amounts and disclosures in the consolidated financial statements. The procedures selected depend on the auditor's judgment, including the assessment of the risks of material misstatement of the consolidated financial statements, whether due to fraud or error. In making those risk assessments, the auditor considers internal control relevant to the entity's preparation and fair presentation of the consolidated financial statements in order to design audit procedures that are appropriate in the circumstances, but not for the purpose of expressing an opinion on the effectiveness of the entity's internal control. Accordingly, we express no such opinion. An audit also includes evaluating the appropriateness of accounting policies used and the reasonableness of significant accounting estimates made by management, as well as evaluating the overall presentation of the consolidated financial statements. We believe that the audit evidence we have obtained is sufficient and appropriate to provide a basis for our audit opinion.

Opinion

In our opinion, based on our audit and the report of the other auditors, the consolidated financial statements referred to above present fairly, in all material respects, the financial position of ABC Company and its subsidiaries as of December 31, 20X1 and 20X0, and the results of their operations and their cash flows for the year then ended in accordance with accounting principles generally accepted in the United States of America.

[*Auditor's signature*]
[*Auditor's city and state*]
[*Date of the auditor's report*]

3.2 Assumption of Responsibility

When the group auditor decides to assume responsibility for the work of a component auditor, no reference to the component auditor is made in the auditor's report.

Question 1   MCQ-09769

According to GAAS, which of the following procedures is *not* required when the group auditor decides to make reference to the component auditor in the auditor's report on the group financial statements?

1. The group auditor should be satisfied with the independence of the component auditor.

2. The component auditor's report is not restricted.

3. The group auditor should be satisfied with the competence of the component auditor.

4. The group auditor should determine the type of work to be performed on the financial information of the components.

---

4 Emphasis-of-Matter, Other-Matter, Explanatory, and Critical Audit Matters Paragraphs

4.1 Emphasis-of-Matter Paragraphs

An emphasis-of-matter paragraph is included in the auditor's report when required by GAAS or at the auditor's discretion. An emphasis-of-matter paragraph is used when referring to a matter that is appropriately presented or disclosed in the financial statements and is of such importance that it is fundamental to the users' understanding of the financial statements.

4.1.1 Report Requirements

When an emphasis-of-matter paragraph is included in the auditor's report, the auditor should:

- place the emphasis-of-matter paragraph immediately after the opinion paragraph;

- use the heading "Emphasis of Matter" or other appropriate heading;

- describe the matter and the location of relevant disclosures; and

- state that the auditor's report is not modified with respect to the matter emphasized.

4.1.2 Lack of Consistency—Justified (Acceptable/Justified Change in Accounting Principle)

Consistency is implied in the auditor's report. *If a material change in GAAP has occurred* between periods and such change is justified, the auditor should *add an emphasis-of-matter paragraph* to the auditor's opinion describing the change and referring the reader to the note describing the change in detail.

4.2 Other-Matter Paragraphs

An other-matter paragraph is included in the auditor's report when required by GAAS or at the auditor's discretion. Other-matter paragraphs refer to matters other than those presented or disclosed in the financial statements that are relevant to the users' understanding of the audit, the auditor's responsibilities, or the auditor's report.

4.2.1 Report Requirements

When an other-matter paragraph is included in the auditor's report, the auditor should:

■ place the other-matter paragraph immediately after the opinion paragraph and after any emphasis-of-matter paragraph;

■ use the heading "Other Matter" or other appropriate heading; and

■ describe the matter and the location of relevant disclosures.

4.2.2 Alert That Restricts the Use of the Auditor's Written Communication

The auditor may be required by GAAS or may decide that it is necessary to include language in the auditor's report (or other written communication) that restricts the use of the auditor's written communication. In the auditor's report, such language is included in an *other-matter paragraph*.

4.3 Explanatory Paragraphs

An explanatory paragraph is included in the auditor's report when required by PCAOB auditing standards or at the auditor's discretion. The inclusion of an explanatory paragraph in the auditor's report does not affect the auditor's opinion.

4.3.1 Report Requirements

When an explanatory paragraph is included in the auditor's report, the auditor generally should place the explanatory paragraph immediately after the opinion paragraph and describe the matter.

4.4 Critical Audit Matters (Issuers Only)

The auditor's report for audits of issuers must include any critical audit matters (CAMs) arising from the current period's audit of the financial statements, or state that the auditor determined that there were no CAMs.

A critical audit matter is a matter that was communicated or required to be communicated to the audit committee and that:

1. relates to accounts or disclosures that are material to the financial statements; and

2. involved especially challenging, subjective, or complex auditor judgment.

4.4.1 Reporting Requirements

For each CAM identified, the audit report should include:

- **identification** of the CAM;

- description of the **principal** considerations that led the auditor to determine that the matter was a CAM;

- description of how the CAM was **addressed** in the audit; and

- reference to the relevant financial statement accounts or **disclosures**.

Question 2   MCQ-09768

Which of the following circumstances requires the use of an emphasis-of-matter paragraph?

1. An alert in the audit report restricts the use of the audit report.

2. Prior to the audit report date, the auditor identifies a material inconsistency in other information that is included in the document containing audited financial statements that management refuses to revise.

3. The financial statements are prepared in accordance with a special purpose framework.

4. The auditor chooses to report on supplementary information presented with the financial statements in the auditor's report, rather than in a separate report.

---

5 GAAP Issues: Qualified or Adverse Opinion

The auditor uses professional judgment to determine whether to issue a qualified opinion or an adverse opinion when audit evidence indicates that there is material misstatement of the financial statements.

Materiality of Problem		Financial Statements Are Materially Misstated (GAAP Issues)	Inability to Obtain Sufficient Appropriate Audit Evidence (GAAS Issues)
None or immaterial	=	Unmodified	Unmodified
Material but not pervasive	=	Qualified opinion	Qualified opinion
Material and pervasive	=	Adverse opinion	Disclaimer of opinion

5.1 Qualified Opinion

A qualified opinion should be expressed when the auditor concludes that misstatements, individually or in the aggregate, are material but not pervasive to the financial statements.

5.2 Adverse Opinion

An adverse opinion should be expressed when the auditor concludes that misstatements, individually or in the aggregate, are both material and pervasive to the financial statements.

5.3 Form and Content of Auditor's Report

Nonissuers: When the auditor expresses a qualified or adverse opinion due to a material misstatement of the financial statements, the "Auditor's Responsibility" paragraph is modified and the auditor's report includes a "Basis for Modification" paragraph and a "Qualified Opinion" or "Adverse Opinion" paragraph, as appropriate.

Issuers: When the auditor expresses a qualified or adverse opinion due to material misstatement of the financial statements, the auditor's report will include an additional paragraph immediately following the opinion paragraph and the opinion paragraph will be modified. The auditor is not required to report critical audit matters in the auditor's report when the auditor expresses an adverse opinion.

5.3.1 Qualified Opinion—GAAP Problem (Nonissuer)

Independent Auditor's Report

[*Appropriate Addressee*]

We have audited the accompanying financial statements of ABC Company, which comprise the balance sheets as of December 31, 20X1 and 20X0, and the related statements of income, changes in stockholders' equity, and cash flows for the years then ended, and the related notes to the financial statements.

Management's Responsibility for the Financial Statements

Management is responsible for the preparation and fair presentation of these financial statements in accordance with accounting principles generally accepted in the United States of America; this includes the design, implementation, and maintenance of internal control relevant to the preparation and fair presentation of financial statements that are free from material misstatement whether due to fraud or error.

Auditor's Responsibility

Our responsibility is to express an opinion on these financial statements based on our audits. We conducted our audits in accordance with auditing standards generally accepted in the United States of America. Those standards require that we plan and perform the audit to obtain reasonable assurance about whether the financial statements are free from material misstatement.

An audit involves performing procedures to obtain audit evidence about the amounts and disclosures in the financial statements. The procedures selected depend on the auditor's judgment, including the assessment of the risks of material misstatement of the financial statements, whether due to fraud or error. In making those risk assessments, the auditor considers internal control relevant to the entity's preparation and fair presentation of the financial statements in order to design audit procedures that are appropriate in the circumstances, but not for the purpose of expressing an opinion on the effectiveness of the entity's internal control. Accordingly, we express no such opinion. An audit also includes evaluating the appropriateness of accounting policies used and the reasonableness of significant accounting estimates made by management, as well as evaluating the overall presentation of the financial statements.

We believe that the audit evidence we have obtained is sufficient and appropriate to provide a basis for our qualified audit opinion.

Basis for Qualified Opinion

The Company has stated inventories at cost in the accompanying balance sheets. Accounting principles generally accepted in the United States of America require inventories to be stated at the lower of cost or market. If the Company stated inventories at the lower of cost or market, a write down of $XXX and $XXX would have been required as of December 31, 20X1 and 20X0, respectively. Accordingly, costs of sales would have increased by $XXX and $XXX, and net income, income taxes, and stockholders' equity would have been reduced by $XXX, $XXX, and $XXX, and $XXX, $XXX, and $XXX, as of and for the years ended December 31, 20X1 and 20X0, respectively.

Qualified Opinion

In our opinion, except for the effects of the matter described in the Basis for Qualified Opinion paragraph, the financial statements referred to above present fairly, in all material respects, the financial position of ABC Company as of December 31, 20X1 and 20X0, and the results of its operations and its cash flows for the years then ended in accordance with accounting principles generally accepted in the United States of America.

[*Auditor's signature*]
[*Auditor's city and state*]
[*Date of the auditor's report*]

5.3.2 Adverse Opinion (Nonissuer)

Independent Auditor's Report

[*Appropriate Addressee*]

We have audited the accompanying consolidated financial statements of ABC Company and its subsidiaries, which comprise the balance sheet as of December 31, 20X1, and the related consolidated statements of income, changes in stockholders' equity, and cash flows for the year then ended, and the related notes to the financial statements.

Management's Responsibility for the Financial Statements

Management is responsible for the preparation and fair presentation of these consolidated financial statements in accordance with accounting principles generally accepted in the United States of America; this includes the design, implementation, and maintenance of internal control relevant to the preparation and fair presentation of consolidated financial statements that are free from material misstatement whether due to fraud or error.

Auditor's Responsibility

Our responsibility is to express an opinion on these consolidated financial statements based on our audits. We conducted our audits in accordance with auditing standards generally accepted in the United States of America. Those standards require that we plan and perform the audit to obtain reasonable assurance about whether the financial statements are free from material misstatement.

An audit involves performing procedures to obtain audit evidence about the amounts and disclosures in the consolidated financial statements. The procedures selected depend on the auditor's judgment, including the assessment of the risks of material misstatement of the consolidated financial statements, whether due to fraud or error. In making those risk assessments, the auditor considers internal control relevant to the entity's preparation and fair presentation of the consolidated financial statements in order to design audit procedures that are appropriate in the circumstances, but not for the purpose of expressing an opinion on the effectiveness of the entity's internal control. Accordingly, we express no such opinion. An audit also includes evaluating the appropriateness of accounting policies used and the reasonableness of significant accounting estimates made by management, as well as evaluating the overall presentation of the consolidated financial statements.

We believe that the audit evidence we have obtained is sufficient and appropriate to provide a basis for our adverse audit opinion.

Basis for Adverse Opinion

As described in Note X, the Company has not consolidated the financial statements of subsidiary XYZ Company that it acquired during 20X1 because it has not yet been able to ascertain the fair value of certain of the subsidiary's material assets and liabilities at the acquisition date. This investment is therefore accounted for on a cost basis by the Company. Under accounting principles generally accepted in the United States of America, the subsidiary should have been consolidated because it is controlled by the Company. Had XYZ Company been consolidated, many elements in the accompanying consolidated financial statements would have been materially affected. The effects on the consolidated financial statements of the failure to consolidate have not been determined.

Adverse Opinion

In our opinion, because of the significance of the matter discussed in the Basis for Adverse Opinion paragraph, the consolidated financial statements referred to above do not present fairly the financial position of ABC Company and its subsidiaries as of December 31, 20X1, or the results of their operations or their cash flows for the year then ended.

[*Auditor's signature*]
[*Auditor's city and state*]
[*Date of the auditor's report*]

6 GAAS Issues—Qualified Opinion or Disclaimer

The auditor uses professional judgment to determine whether to issue a qualified opinion or a disclaimer of opinion due to a limitation on the scope of the audit. A scope limitation occurs when the auditor is unable to obtain sufficient appropriate audit evidence to conclude that the financial statements are free of material misstatement.

Materiality of Problem		Financial Statements Are Materially Misstated (GAAP Issues)	Inability to Obtain Sufficient Appropriate Audit Evidence (GAAS Issues)
None or immaterial	=	Unmodified	Unmodified
Material but not pervasive	=	Qualified opinion	Qualified opinion
Material and pervasive	=	Adverse opinion	Disclaimer of opinion

6.1 Qualified Opinion

A qualified opinion due to a GAAS issue should be expressed when the auditor is unable to obtain sufficient appropriate audit evidence on which to base an opinion and the auditor concludes that the possible effects of any undetected misstatements could be material but not pervasive.

6.2 Disclaimer of Opinion

A disclaimer of opinion should be expressed when the auditor is unable to obtain sufficient appropriate audit evidence on which to base an opinion and the auditor concludes that the possible effects of any undetected misstatements could be both material and pervasive.

6.3 Form and Content of the Auditor's Report

Nonissuer: When the auditor expresses a qualified opinion or disclaimer of opinion due to scope limitation, the Auditor's Responsibility paragraph is modified and the auditor's report will include a Basis for Modification paragraph and a Qualified Opinion or Disclaimer of Opinion paragraph, as appropriate. A disclaimer of opinion will also include a modification to the introductory paragraph of the auditor's report.

Issuer: When the auditor expresses a qualified opinion or disclaimer of opinion, a paragraph immediately following the opinion paragraph is added and the opinion paragraph is modified. A qualified opinion and disclaimer of opinion will include modified language in the basis for opinion section. The auditor is not required to report critical audit matters in the auditor's report when the auditor expresses a disclaimer of opinion.

6.3.1 Qualified Opinion—GAAS Problem (Nonissuer)

Independent Auditor's Report

[*Appropriate Addressee*]

We have audited the accompanying financial statements of ABC Company, which comprise the balance sheets as of December 31, 20X1, and the related statements of income, changes in stockholders' equity, and cash flows for the year then ended, and the related notes to the financial statements.

Management's Responsibility for the Financial Statements

Management is responsible for the preparation and fair presentation of these financial statements in accordance with accounting principles generally accepted in the United States of America; this includes the design, implementation, and maintenance of internal control relevant to the preparation and fair presentation of financial statements that are free from material misstatement whether due to fraud or error.

Auditor's Responsibility

Our responsibility is to express an opinion on these financial statements based on our audits. We conducted our audits in accordance with auditing standards generally accepted in the United States of America. Those standards require that we plan and perform the audit to obtain reasonable assurance about whether the financial statements are free from material misstatement.

An audit involves performing procedures to obtain audit evidence about the amounts and disclosures in the financial statements. The procedures selected depend on the auditor's judgment, including the assessment of the risks of material misstatement of the financial statements, whether due to fraud or error. In making those risk assessments, the auditor considers internal control relevant to the entity's preparation and fair presentation of the financial statements in order to design audit procedures that are appropriate in the circumstances, but not for the purpose of expressing an opinion on the effectiveness of the entity's internal control. Accordingly, we express no such opinion. An audit also includes evaluating the appropriateness of accounting policies used and the reasonableness of significant accounting estimates made by management, as well as evaluating the overall presentation of the financial statements.

We believe that the audit evidence we have obtained is sufficient and appropriate to provide a basis for our qualified audit opinion.

Basis for Qualified Opinion

ABC Company's investment in XYZ Company, a foreign affiliate acquired during the year and accounted for under the equity method is carried at $XXX on the balance sheet at December 31, 20X1, and ABC Company's share of XYZ Company's net income of $XXX is included in ABC Company's net income for the year then ended. We were unable to obtain sufficient appropriate audit evidence about the carrying amount of ABC Company's investment in XYZ Company as of December 31, 20X1 and ABC Company's share of XYZ Company's net income for the year then ended because we were denied access to the financial information, management, and the auditors of XYZ Company. Consequently, we were unable to determine whether any adjustments to these amounts were necessary.

Qualified Opinion

In our opinion, except for the possible effects of the matter described in the Basis for Qualified Opinion paragraph, the financial statements referred to above present fairly, in all material respects, the financial position of ABC Company as of December 31, 20X1, and the results of its operations and its cash flows for the year then ended in accordance with accounting principles generally accepted in the United States of America.

[*Auditor's signature*]
[*Auditor's city and state*]
[*Date of the auditor's report*]

6.3.2 Disclaimer of Opinion (Nonissuer)

Independent Auditor's Report

[Appropriate Addressee]

We were engaged to audit the accompanying financial statements of ABC Company, which comprise the balance sheets as of December 31, 20X1, and the related statements of income, changes in stockholders' equity, and cash flows for the year then ended, and the related notes to the financial statements.

Management's Responsibility for the Financial Statements

Management is responsible for the preparation and fair presentation of these financial statements in accordance with accounting principles generally accepted in the United States of America; this includes the design, implementation, and maintenance of internal control relevant to the preparation and fair presentation of financial statements that are free from material misstatement whether due to fraud or error.

Auditor's Responsibility

Our responsibility is to express an opinion on these financial statements based on conducting the audit in accordance with auditing standards generally accepted in the United States of America. Because of the matters described in the Basis for Disclaimer of Opinion paragraph, however, we were not able to obtain sufficient appropriate audit evidence to provide a basis for an audit opinion.

Basis for Disclaimer of Opinion

We were not engaged as auditors of the Company until after December 31, 20X1, and, therefore, did not observe the counting of physical inventories at the beginning or end of the year. We were unable to satisfy ourselves by other auditing procedures concerning the inventory held at December 31, 20X1, which is stated in the balance sheet at $XXX. In addition, the introduction of a new computerized accounts receivable system in September 20X1 resulted in numerous misstatements in accounts receivable. As of the date of our audit report, management was still in the process of rectifying the system deficiencies and correcting the misstatements. We were unable to confirm or verify by alternative means accounts receivable included in the balance sheet at a total amount of $XXX at December 31, 20X1. As a result of these matters, we were unable to determine whether any adjustments might have been found necessary in respect of recorded or unrecorded inventories and accounts receivable, and the elements making up the statements of income, changes in stockholder's equity, and cash flows.

Disclaimer of Opinion

Because of the significance of the matters described in the Basis for Disclaimer of Opinion paragraph, we have not been able to obtain sufficient appropriate audit evidence to provide a basis for an audit opinion. Accordingly, we do not express an opinion on these financial statements.

[Auditor's signature]
[Auditor's city and state]
[Date of the auditor's report]

Under which of the following situations would the expression of a disclaimer of opinion be inappropriate?

1. The entity's going concern disclosures are adequate.

2. Management refuses to allow the auditor to send a letter of inquiry to their attorneys.

3. The auditor is not independent.

4. Management fails to disclose a significant subsequent event.

7 Comparative Financial Statements

7.1 Change in Opinion

A prior opinion may be changed. The auditor should update (i.e., either reaffirm or change) the opinion on any previously issued financial statements shown in comparative statements.

If the updated opinion differs from the previous opinion, the auditor should disclose the reason(s) in an *emphasis-of-matter or other-matter paragraph* (nonissuer) or *explanatory paragraph* (issuer) that discloses the following:

- **D**ate of the previous auditor's report.
- **O**pinion type previously issued.
- **R**eason for the prior opinion.
- **C**hanges that have occurred.
- **S**tatement that "opinion ... is different."

7.1.1 Sample Other-Matter Paragraph—Updating Prior Opinion

Other Matter

In our report dated March 1, 20X1, we expressed an opinion that the 20X0 financial statements did not fairly present the financial position, results of operations, and cash flows of ABC Company in accordance with accounting principles generally accepted in the United States of America because of two departures from such principles: (1) ABC Company carried its property, plant, and equipment at appraisal values, and provided for depreciation on the basis of such values; and (2) ABC Company did not provide for deferred income taxes with respect to differences between income for financial reporting purposes and taxable income. As described in Note X, the Company has changed its method of accounting for these items and restated its 20X0 financial statements to conform with accounting principles generally accepted in the United States of America. Accordingly, our present opinion on the restated 20X0 financial statements, as presented herein, is different from that expressed in our previous report.

7.2 Different Opinions

Some comparative reports will have different opinions for each year presented.
Depending upon the situation, the appropriate paragraphs will be modified.

7.2.1 Report on Comparative Financial Statements— Different Opinions (Nonissuer)

Independent Auditor's Report

[*Appropriate Addressee*]

We have audited the accompanying financial statements of ABC Company, which comprise the balance sheets as of December 31, 20X1 and 20X0, and the related statements of income, changes in stockholders' equity, and cash flows for the years then ended, and the related notes to the financial statements.

Management's Responsibility for the Financial Statements

Management is responsible for the preparation and fair presentation of these financial statements in accordance with accounting principles generally accepted in the United States of America; this includes the design, implementation, and maintenance of internal control relevant to the preparation and fair presentation of financial statements that are free from material misstatement whether due to fraud or error.

Auditor's Responsibility

Our responsibility is to express an opinion on these financial statements based on our audits. We conducted our audit in accordance with auditing standards generally accepted in the United States of America. Those standards require that we plan and perform the audit to obtain reasonable assurance about whether the financial statements are free from material misstatement.

An audit involves performing procedures to obtain audit evidence about the amounts and disclosures in the financial statements. The procedures selected depend on the auditor's judgment, including the assessment of the risks of material misstatement of the financial statements, whether due to fraud or error. In making those risk assessments, the auditor considers internal control relevant to the entity's preparation and fair presentation of the financial statements in order to design audit procedures that are appropriate in the circumstances, but not for the purpose of expressing an opinion on the effectiveness of the entity's internal control. Accordingly, we express no such opinion. An audit also includes evaluating the appropriateness of accounting policies used and the reasonableness of significant accounting estimates made by management, as well as evaluating the overall presentation of the financial statements.

We believe that the audit evidence we have obtained is sufficient and appropriate to provide a basis for our qualified audit opinion.

Basis for Qualified Opinion

The company has excluded, from property and debt in the accompanying 20X1 balance sheet, certain capital lease obligations that were entered into in 20X1 which, in our opinion, should be capitalized in accordance with accounting principles generally accepted in the United States of America. If these lease obligations were capitalized, property would be increased by $XXX, long-term debt by $XXX, and retained earnings by $XXX as of December 31, 20X1, and net income and earnings per share would be increased (decreased) by $XXX and $XXX, respectively, for the year then ended.

Qualified Opinion

In our opinion, except for the effects on the 20X1 financial statements of not capitalizing certain lease obligations as described in the Basis for Qualified Opinion paragraph, the financial statements referred to above present fairly, in all material respects, the financial position of ABC Company as of December 31, 20X1 and 20X0, and the results of its operations and its cash flows for the years then ended in accordance with accounting principles generally accepted in the United States of America.

[*Auditor's signature*]
[*Auditor's city and state*]
[*Date of the auditor's report*]

In Year 1, Randall, CPA, issued a qualified opinion on the financial statements of Celadon Industries, a nonissuer, due to the improper recording of lease obligations. During Year 2, Celadon restated the Year 1 financial statements to correct the error, and now plans to issue comparative financial statements for Year 1 and Year 2. Which of the following is true about Randall's report on the comparative financial statements?

1. Randall may not change the prior opinion, but may add an other-matter paragraph to the report indicating that the previous error has been corrected.

2. Randall may revise the prior opinion, but must include an emphasis-of-matter or other-matter paragraph describing the situation.

3. Randall may not change the prior opinion, and should not issue a report on the comparative financial statements.

4. Randall may revise the prior opinion and need not make mention of the change, as long as the comparative financial statements include the revised statements (and not the original statements) for Year 1.

8 Required Auditor Reporting of Certain Audit Participants

8.1 Filing of Form AP

An issuer must file Form AP with the PCAOB for each audit report issued. This form includes information about the audit, such as:

- Name of the firm.
- Name of the issuer whose financial statements are audited.
- Date of the audit report.
- The end date of the most recent period's financial statements identified in the audit report.
- The name of the engagement partner on the most recent period's audit and his/her current and prior ID number(s).
- The city and state (or city and country) of the office of the firm issuing the audit report.
- Whether the audit report is dual-dated.
- Whether other accounting firms participated in the audit.
- Whether the firm divided responsibility for the audit.
- Signature of partner or authorized officer.

Form AP must be filed by the 35th day after the audit report is first filed in a document with the SEC or within 10 days if the audit report is included in a registration statement.

8.2 Optional Inclusions

Although not required, the auditor of an issuer may elect to include in the auditor's report information regarding the engagement partner and/or other accounting firms participating in the audit.

1 Integrated Audits of Issuers

PCAOB standards, which apply to issuers, require that auditors perform an "integrated audit," auditing internal control in conjunction with the audit of the financial statements. The Dodd-Frank Act amended this rule, providing that integrated audits are required only for large accelerated filers and accelerated filers.

2 Integrated Audits of Nonissuers

SASs allow an auditor to audit and report on a nonissuer's internal control over financial reporting that is integrated with a financial statement audit. The rules governing integrated audits of nonissuers are very similar to the rules for issuers.

3 Impact on Tests of Controls

In both issuer and nonissuer integrated audits, tests of controls should be designed to provide sufficient appropriate evidence to support both the opinion on internal control and the control risk assessment in the financial statement audit.

3.1 Top-Down Approach

A top-down approach is used to select the controls to test. The auditor should:

- Evaluate overall risk at the financial statement level.
- Consider controls at the entity level.
- Focus tests of controls on accounts, disclosures, and assertions for which there is a reasonable possibility of material misstatement.

Question 1   MCQ-09864

In an integrated audit of an issuer, which of the following most likely would be considered an entity-level control?

1. The auditor's adherence to a system of quality control.

2. Management's procedures used to initiate, authorize, and record journal entries into the general ledger.

3. An aging schedule that is prepared by the accounts receivable department.

4. Upon receiving checks from customers by mail, an employee prepares a duplicate listing of checks received.

1 Communications With Management and Those Charged With Governance

The auditor is not required to search for control deficiencies or significant deficiencies in a financial statement audit only, but those that are identified should be communicated.

- Control deficiencies, significant deficiencies, and material weaknesses should be communicated to management in writing.

- Significant deficiencies and material weaknesses must also be communicated to the audit committee in writing.

- For issuers, material weaknesses should be communicated to management and the audit committee before the issuance of the auditor's report on internal control.

- For nonissuers, communication of significant deficiencies and material weaknesses should be made by the report release date and communication of control deficiencies should be made within 60 days of the report release date.

Question 1   MCQ-09064

With respect to the expression of an opinion regarding whether a client maintained effective internal control over financial reporting:

1. The auditor of a nonissuer may express an opinion as a result of an audit engagement.

2. The auditor of a nonissuer may express an opinion as a result of a financial statement audit.

3. The auditor of a nonissuer must express an opinion in every financial statement audit.

4. The auditor of a nonissuer must express an opinion whenever significant deficiencies or material weaknesses are noted.

2 Opinion on Internal Control

The auditor must express an opinion on the company's internal control over financial reporting in an integrated audit.

2.1 Separate or Combined Reports

This report may be combined with the report on the financial statements, or it may be presented separately. If separate reports are issued, each report should contain an explanatory paragraph making reference to the other report.

2.1.1 Sample Combined Report (Issuer)

Report of Independent Registered Public Accounting Firm

To the shareholders and the board of directors of W Company:

Opinions on the Financial Statements and Internal Control Over Financial Reporting

We have audited the accompanying balance sheets of W Company (the "Company") as of December 31, 20X8 and 20X7, and the related statements of income, comprehensive income, stockholders' equity, and cash flows for each of the years in the two-year period ended December 31, 20X8, and the related notes [*and schedules*] (collectively referred to as the "financial statements"). We also have audited the Company's internal control over financial reporting as of December 31, 20X8, based on [*identify control criteria, for example, "criteria established in Internal Control-Integrated Framework: (20XX) issued by the Committee of Sponsoring Organizations of the Treadway Commission (COSO)"*].

In our opinion, the financial statements referred to above present fairly, in all material respects, the financial position of the Company as of December 31, 20X8 and 20X7, and the results of its operations and its cash flows for each of the years in the two-year period ended December 31, 20X8, in conformity with accounting principles generally accepted in the United States of America. Also in our opinion, the Company maintained, in all material respects, effective internal control over financial reporting as of December 31, 20X8, based on [*identify control criteria, for example, "criteria established in Internal Control-Integrated Framework: (20XX) issued by COSO"*].

Basis for Opinion

The Company's management is responsible for these financial statements, for maintaining effective internal control over financial reporting, and for its assessment of the effectiveness of internal control over financial reporting, included in the accompanying [title of management's report]. Our responsibility is to express an opinion on the Company's financial statements and an opinion on the Company's internal control over financial reporting based on our audits. We are a public accounting firm registered with the Public Company Accounting Oversight Board (United States) (PCAOB) and are required to be independent with respect to the Company in accordance with the U.S. federal securities laws and the applicable rules and regulations of the Securities and Exchange Commission and the PCAOB.

We conducted our audits in accordance with the standards of the PCAOB. Those standards require that we plan and perform the audits to obtain reasonable assurance about whether the financial statements are free of material misstatement, whether due to error or fraud, and whether effective internal control over financial reporting was maintained in all material respects.

(continued on next page)

(continued)

Our audits of the financial statements included performing procedures to assess the risks of material misstatement of the financial statements, whether due to error or fraud, and performing procedures that respond to those risks. Such procedures included examining, on a test basis, evidence regarding the amounts and disclosures in the financial statements. Our audits also included evaluating the accounting principles used and significant estimates made by management, as well as evaluating the overall presentation of the financial statements. Our audit of internal control over financial reporting included obtaining an understanding of internal control over financial reporting, assessing the risk that a material weakness exists, and testing and evaluating the design and operating effectiveness of internal control based on the assessed risk. Our audits also included performing such other procedures as we considered necessary in the circumstances. We believe that our audits provide a reasonable basis for our opinions.

Definition and Limitations of Internal Control Over Financial Reporting

A company's internal control over financial reporting is a process designed to provide reasonable assurance regarding the reliability of financial reporting and the preparation of financial statements for external purposes in accordance with generally accepted accounting principles. A company's internal control over financial reporting includes those policies and procedures that (1) pertain to the maintenance of records that, in reasonable detail, accurately and fairly reflect the transactions and dispositions of the assets of the company; (2) provide reasonable assurance that transactions are recorded as necessary to permit preparation of financial statements in accordance with generally accepted accounting principles, and that receipts and expenditures of the company are being made only in accordance with authorizations of management and directors of the company; and (3) provide reasonable assurance regarding prevention or timely detection of unauthorized acquisition, use, or disposition of the company's assets that could have a material effect on the financial statements.

Because of its inherent limitations, internal control over financial reporting may not prevent or detect misstatements. Also, projections of any evaluation of effectiveness to future periods are subject to the risk that controls may become inadequate because of changes in conditions, or that the degree of compliance with the policies or procedures may deteriorate.

Critical Audit Matters

[*Include critical audit matters*]

[*Signature*]

We have served as the Company's auditor since [year].

[*City and State or Country*]

[*Date*]

2.1.2 Sample Combined Report (Nonissuer)

Independent Auditor's Report

[*Appropriate addressee*]

We have audited the financial statements of W Company, which comprise the balance sheet as of December 31, 20XX, and the related statements of income, changes in stockholder's equity, and cash flows for the year then ended, and the related notes to the financial statements. We also have audited W Company's internal control over financial reporting as of December 31, 20XX, based on [*identify criteria*].

Management's Responsibility for the Financial Statements and Internal Control Over Financial Reporting

Management is responsible for the preparation and fair presentation of these financial statements in accordance with accounting principles generally accepted in the United States of America, for maintaining internal control over financial reporting including the design, implementation, and maintenance of controls; this includes the design, implementation, and maintenance of effective internal control over financial reporting relevant to the preparation and fair presentation of these financial statements that are free from material misstatement, whether due to error of fraud. Management is also responsible for its assertion about the effectiveness of internal control over financial reporting, included in the accompanying [*title of management's report*].

Auditor's Responsibility

Our responsibility is to express an opinion on these financial statements and an opinion on W Company's internal control over financial reporting based on our audits. We conducted our audit of the financial statements in accordance with auditing standards generally accepted in the United States of America and our audit of internal control over financial reporting in accordance with attestation standards established by the American Institute of Certified Public Accountants. Those standards require that we plan and perform the audits to obtain reasonable assurance about whether the financial statements are free of material misstatement and whether effective internal control over financial reporting was maintained in all material respects.

An audit of financial statements involves performing procedures to obtain audit evidence about the amounts and disclosures in the financial statements. The procedures selected depend on the auditor's judgment, including assessment of the risks of material misstatement of the financial statements, whether due to fraud or error. In making those risk assessments, the auditor considers internal control relevant to the entity's preparation and fair presentation of the financial statements in order to design audit procedures that are appropriate in the circumstances. An audit of internal control over financial reporting involves obtaining an understanding of internal control over financial reporting, assessing the risk that a material weakness exists, and testing and evaluating the design and operating effectiveness of internal control over financial reporting based on the assessed risk, and performing such other procedures as we considered necessary in the circumstances.

We believe that the audit evidence we obtained is sufficient and appropriate to provide a basis for our audit opinions.

Definitions and Inherent Limitations of Internal Control Over Financial Reporting

An entity's internal control over financial reporting is a process effected by those charged with governance, management, and other personnel, designed to provide reasonable assurance regarding the preparation of reliable financial statements in accordance with [*applicable financial reporting framework, such as accounting principles generally accepted in the United States of America*]. An entity's internal control over financial reporting includes those policies and procedures that (1) pertain to the maintenance of records that, in reasonable detail, accurately and fairly reflect the transactions and dispositions of the assets of the entity; (2) provide reasonable assurance that transactions are recorded as necessary to permit preparation of financial statements in accordance with [*applicable financial reporting framework, such as accounting principles generally accepted in the United States of America*], and that receipts and expenditures of the entity are being made only in accordance with authorizations of management and those charged with governance; and (3) provide reasonable assurance regarding prevention, or timely detection and correction of unauthorized acquisition, use, or disposition of the entity's assets that could have a material effect on the financial statements.

Because of its inherent limitations, internal control over financial reporting may not prevent, or detect and correct misstatements. Also, projections of any evaluation of effectiveness to future periods are subject to the risk that controls may become inadequate because of changes in conditions, or that the degree of compliance with the policies or procedures may deteriorate.

(continued on next page)

(continued)

Opinions

In our opinion, the financial statements referred to above present fairly, in all material respects, the financial position of W Company as of December 31, 20XX, and the results of its operations and its cash flows for the year then ended in accordance with accounting principles generally accepted in the United States of America. Also in our opinion, W Company maintained, in all material respects, effective internal control over financial reporting as of December 31, 20XX, based on [*identify criteria*].

[*Auditor's signature*]
[*Auditor's city and state*]
[*Date of the auditor's report*]

2.2   Modified Audit Opinions

2.2.1   Scope Limitation

A scope limitation requires the auditor to disclaim an opinion or to withdraw from the engagement.

2.2.2   Material Weakness

A material weakness requires the auditor to issue an adverse opinion. The adverse opinion should include:

■ the definition of material weakness.

■ a statement that a material weakness has been identified.

■ an identification of the material weakness described in management's own assessment of internal control.

If the material weakness is not included in management's assessment, the report should state this and should include a description of the material weakness.

2.2.3   Absence of Control Deficiencies or Significant Deficiencies

The auditor should not report the absence of control deficiencies or significant deficiencies.

Question 2	MCQ-09861

During an integrated audit, an auditor uncovers one control deficiency in internal control such that there is a reasonable possibility that a material misstatement of the entity's financial statements will not be prevented, or detected and corrected on a timely basis. In this situation, the auditor should issue an opinion on internal control that is:

1. Unmodified

2. Qualified

3. Adverse

4. A disclaimer

1 Statements on Standards for Attestation Engagements

Statements on Standards for Attestation Engagements (SSAE) apply to engagements in which a practitioner is engaged to issue, or does issue, an examination, review, or agreed-upon procedures report on subject matter (or an assertion thereon) that is another party's responsibility. Independence is required.

1.1 Levels of Reports

There are three levels of reports that may be issued on the assertion or the associated subject matter:

1. Examination (reasonable assurance, with positive opinion)

2. Review (limited assurance, with conclusion)

3. Agreed-upon procedures (no assurance, with list of findings)

Report Type			
Attestation Service	*Examination*	*Review*	*Agreed-Upon Procedures*
Agreed-upon procedures			✓
Prospective financial statements	✓		✓
Pro forma financial statements	✓	✓	
Compliance	✓		✓
MD&A	✓	✓	
Service organizations	✓		

Note that preparations and compilations are also allowed for prospective financial statements. However, with the issuance of SSAE 18, preparations and compilations of prospective financial statements are no longer addressed in the attestation standards and are instead governed by the SSARS standards.

2 "Agreed-Upon" Procedures Engagements

The practitioner is engaged to report findings using specific, agreed-upon procedures. Required conditions:

- **I**ndependence of the practitioner.

- **A**greement of parties—the practitioner and specified parties agree regarding procedures to be performed, the criteria to be used in the determination of findings, and any materiality limits used for reporting.

- **M**easurability and consistency—subject matter should be capable of reasonably consistent measurement, procedures should be expected to result in reasonably consistent findings, and evidential matter to support the report should be expected to exist.

- **S**ufficiency of procedures—specified parties take responsibility for the sufficiency of procedures for their purposes.

- **U**se of the report is restricted to specified parties.

- **R**esponsibility for subject matter. Either:
  - the client is responsible for (or has a reasonable basis for providing an assertion about) the subject matter; or
  - the client is able to provide evidence of a third party's responsibility for the subject matter.

- **E**ngagements to perform agreed-upon procedures on prospective financial statements.
  - Prospective financial statements must include a summary of significant assumptions.

Question 1   MCQ-09792

Which of the following should a practitioner perform as part of an engagement for agreed-upon procedures in accordance with *Statements on Standards for Attestation Engagements*?

1. Ensure the engagement procedures are comparable to those performed in a compilation.

2. Express a disclaimer of opinion on the subject matter.

3. Express positive assurance on findings of work performed.

4. Disclose responsibility for the sufficiency of procedures.

---

3 Financial Forecasts and Projections

Financial forecasts and projections are prospective financial statements. Allowable engagements for prospective financial statements are preparation, compilation, examination, and agreed-upon procedures. No review engagement is allowed.

Note: SSARS provides guidance for preparations and compilations of financial forecasts and projections. SSAE provides guidance for examinations and agreed-upon procedure engagements of financial forecasts and projections.

3.1   Financial Forecast

Financial forecasts are based on expected conditions and expected courses of action. Financial forecasts are available for general use or may be limited use.

3.1.1   Report on Compilation of a Financial Forecast*

[The responsible party] is responsible for the accompanying financial forecast of XYZ Company, which comprises the forecasted balance sheet as of December 31, 20X2, and the related forecasted statements of income, changes in stockholders' equity, and cash flows for the year then ending, and the related summaries of significant assumptions and accounting policies in accordance with guidelines for the presentation of a financial forecast established by the American Institute of Certified Public Accountants (AICPA). We have performed a compilation engagement in accordance with Statements on Standards for Accounting and Review Services promulgated by the Accounting and Review Services Committee of the AICPA. We did not examine or review the financial forecast nor were we required to perform any procedures to verify the accuracy or completeness of the information provided by management. Accordingly, we do not express an opinion, a conclusion, nor provide any form of assurance on the accompanying financial statements or assumptions.

The forecasted results may not be achieved as there will usually be differences between the forecasted and actual results, because events and circumstances frequently do no occur as expected, and these differences may be material. We have no responsibility to update this report for events and circumstances occurring after the date of this report.

[*Signature of practitioner's firm or accountant, as appropriate*]

[*Practitioner's city and state*]

[*Date of the practitioner's report*]

*With the issuance of SSAE 18, compilations of prospective financial statements are no longer addressed in the attestation standards and are instead governed by AR-C section 80 of the SSARS standards.

3.1.2 Report on Examination of a Financial Forecast

Independent Accountant's Report

[*Appropriate Addressee*]

We have examined the accompanying forecast of XYZ Company, which comprises, the forecasted balance sheet as of December 31, 20XX, and the related forecasted statements of income, stockholders' equity, and cash flows for the year then ending, based on the guidelines for the presentation of a forecast established by the American Institute of Certified Public Accountants. XYZ Company's management is responsible for preparing and presenting the forecast in accordance with the guidelines for the presentation of a forecast established by the American Institute of Certified Public Accountants. Our responsibility is to express an opinion on the forecast based on our examination.

Our examination was conducted in accordance with attestation standards established by the American Institute of Certified Public Accountants. Those standards require that we plan and perform the examination to obtain reasonable assurance about whether the forecast is presented in accordance with the guidelines for the presentation of a forecast established by the American Institute of Certified Public Accountants, in all material respects. An examination involves performing procedures to obtain evidence about the forecast. The nature, timing, and extent of the procedures selected depend on our judgment, including an assessment of the risks of material misstatement of the forecast, whether due to fraud or error. We believe that the evidence we obtained is sufficient and appropriate to provide a reasonable basis for our opinion.

In our opinion, the accompanying forecast is presented, in all material respects, in accordance with the guidelines for the presentation of a forecast established by the American Institute of Certified Public Accountants, and the underlying assumptions are suitably supported and provide a reasonable basis for management's forecast.

There will usually be differences between the forecasted and actual results because events and circumstances frequently do not occur as expected, and those differences may be material. We have no responsibility to update this report for events and circumstances occurring after the date of this report.

[*Practitioner's signature*]
[*Practitioner's city and state*]
[*Date of practitioner's report*]

3.2 Financial Projection

Financial projections are based on hypothetical ("what if") assumptions. Reports on financial projections are restricted use only and cannot be made available for general use.

3.2.1 Report on Compilation of a Financial Projection

The report on the compilation of a financial projection would be similar to the report on the compilation of a financial forecast, except that it would refer to a "financial projection" rather than "financial forecast."

3.2.2 Report on Examination of a Financial Projection

The report on an examination of a financial projection would be similar to the report on the examination of a financial forecast, except it would include a description of the purpose of the projection in the first paragraph, a reference to the hypothetical assumption in the third and fourth paragraphs, and a paragraph restricting the use of the report.

3.3 Prospective Financial Statement (PFS) Summary

General Procedures	Compilation Report*	Examination Report	Agreed-Upon Procedures
Prospective financial statements	Assemble	Evaluate	Apply specific procedures
Responsible party's assumptions	Assemble	Evaluate	Should be included in PFS
Are financial statements and significant assumptions in conformance with AICPA guidelines?	Look for obvious errors	Opinion	Disclaimer
Obtain agreed-upon scope from specified users	—	—	Yes

Reports Include a Statement Regarding:	Compilation Report*	Examination Report	Agreed-Upon Procedures
Identification of PFS	Yes	Yes	Yes
Compliance with AICPA standards	Yes	Yes	Yes
Limitation of scope	Yes	—	Yes
An enumeration of procedures performed	—	—	Yes
A caveat that prospective results may not be achieved	Yes	Yes	Yes
CPA has no responsibility for updating report	Yes	Yes	Yes
Opinion on PFS accordance with AICPA presentation guidelines	—	Yes	—
Limited use of report	Only required for projection	Only required for projection	Yes (always)

*With the issuance of SSAE 18, compilations of prospective financial statements are no longer addressed in the attestation standards and are instead governed by AR-C section 80 of the SSARS standards.

Question 2   MCQ-08129

Which of the following is a prospective financial statement for general use upon which an accountant may appropriately report?

  1. Financial projection

  2. Partial presentation

  3. Pro forma financial statement

  4. Financial forecast

1 Statements on Standards for Accounting and Review Services

SSARS (Statements on Standards for Accounting and Review Services) are issued by the AICPA Accounting and Review Services Committee. SSARS provide guidance with respect to preparations, compilations, and reviews of financial statements of nonissuers.

1.1 Engagement Letter

- All SSARS engagements require a written understanding with management and, when appropriate, those charged with governance, regarding the services to be performed.

- This engagement letter (or other suitable form of written agreement) should be signed by the accountant or the accountant's firm as well as management or those charged with governance.

1.2 Review Engagements

- Independence is required.

- Each page of the financial statements should be marked, "See accountant's review report."

- Review procedures, consisting principally of inquiry and analytical procedures, should be tailored to the specific engagement.

1.2.1 Inquiry

In a review engagement, inquiries should be made about:

- Accounting principles and practices used.

- Procedures for recording, classifying, and summarizing transactions.

- How footnote information is accumulated.

- Changes in business or accounting.

- Subsequent events.

- Whether the financial statements have been prepared and fairly presented in accordance with the applicable financial reporting framework.

- Actions authorized by stockholders or board of directors.

- Unusual or complex situations that may affect the financial statements.

- Significant transactions near the end of the period.

- The status of uncorrected misstatements from previous engagements.

- Material fraud or suspected fraud.

- Significant journal entries and adjustments.

- Communications from regulatory agencies.

- Litigation, claims, and assessments.

- Entity's ability to continue as a going concern (and, if applicable, management's plans to mitigate the going concern issue).
- Whether management has disclosed all known instances of noncompliance with laws and regulations.
- Whether management believes that significant assumptions used for accounting estimates are reasonable.

1.2.2 Analytical Procedures

The accountant should compare current statements with prior statements, compare actual with budgets, and study specific predictable items. The accountant should also compare:

- Financial and relevant nonfinancial information.
- Ratios and indicators with those of other entities in the industry.
- Relationships among elements in the financial statements within the period and with corresponding prior period relationships.

1.2.3 Other Procedures

The accountant should also:

- Obtain an understanding of the client's business.
- Become familiar with the accounting principles used in the client's industry.
- Read the client's financial statements.
- Obtain reports of other accountants who have been engaged to audit or review significant components of the reporting entity.
- Obtain evidence that the financial statements agree or reconcile with accounting records.
- Obtain a representation letter. Management representations should include:
  - Acknowledgment of responsibility to prevent/detect fraud.
  - Knowledge of any material fraud or suspected fraud.
- Issue a review report.

1.3 Compilation Engagements

- No independence is required and no assurance is expressed. Lack of independence must be disclosed in the compilation report. The accountant is permitted, but not required, to disclose the reason(s) for the lack of independence.
- The CPA presents in the form of financial statements, information that is management's representation.

1.3.1 Procedures

■ Obtain knowledge of the client industry's accounting principles practices.

■ Obtain an understanding of the client's business.

■ Read the financial statements to ensure they are free of obvious clerical errors and obvious mistakes related to GAAP.

■ Disclose lack of independence, if applicable.

■ Issue a compilation report.

1.4 Preparation Engagements

■ A preparation does not provide assurance.

■ A preparation is considered a non-attest service, therefore, it does not require a determination of whether the accountant is independent of the entity.

■ In a preparation, the CPA prepares financial statements in accordance with a specified financial reporting framework.

■ The accountant may prepare financial statements that omit disclosures as long as the financial statements clearly indicate the omission.

1.4.1 Procedures

■ Obtain knowledge of the client industry's accounting principles/practices.

■ Obtain an understanding of the client's business.

■ Prepare the financial statements.

■ Ensure a statement on each page at a minimum stating "no assurance is provided" or issue a disclaimer that makes clear no assurance is provided on the financial statements. The accountant or accountant's firm name is not required to be included in prepared financial statements.

1.5 Change in Engagement

■ If the client wishes to change an audit to a compilation or a review, the accountant should:

• Inquire about the reasons for the change (e.g., a change in client requirements, a misunderstanding as to the service to be rendered, a scope restriction).

• Consider the estimated additional cost/effort required to complete the engagement.

■ If the accountant decides that the change in engagement is justified, he/she must comply with standards for a compilation or review and issue an appropriate report.

Question 1
MCQ-04522

Which of the following accounting services may an accountant perform without being required to issue a compilation or review report under Statements on Standards for Accounting and Review Services?

I.   Preparing a working trial balance.

II. Preparing standard monthly journal entries.

   1. I only.

   2. II only.

   3. Both I and II.

   4. Neither I nor II.

Question 2
MCQ-09051

Which of the following procedures would most likely be performed during an engagement to compile the financial statements of a nonissuer?

   1. Read the financial statements and consider whether they are appropriate in form and free from obvious material errors.

   2. Perform inquiry and analytical review procedures.

   3. Obtain a representation letter from management.

   4. Send accounts receivable confirmations.

Question 3
MCQ-09789

A client requests to change an engagement from an audit to a review of financial statements. Which of the following is most likely to be considered by the auditor as an acceptable reason for the change?

   1. Management is unwilling to sign the representation letter because management was not present for the entire period covered by the engagement.

   2. Management does not want the auditor to correspond with legal counsel.

   3. The bank the client is obtaining a loan from has changed the assurance required on the financial statements from positive to negative assurance.

   4. Audit procedures might discover that land is materially overstated.

Question 4   MCQ-09788

Before reissuing a compilation report on the financial statements of a nonissuer for the prior year, the predecessor accountant is required to perform all the following procedures, *except* for:

1. Read the financial statements and the report of the current period.

2. Obtain a letter of representation from management.

3. Compare the prior period financial statements with those issued previously and currently.

4. Obtain a letter from the successor accountants.

---

2 Review of Interim Financial Statements

A review of interim financial statements provides a basis for reporting whether the auditor is aware of any needed material modifications to interim financial information for GAAP conformity. Procedures include inquiries, analytical procedures, and other procedures.

2.1 Procedures

■ The required procedures are:

- **U**nderstanding with the client must be established.

- **L**earn and/or obtain an understanding of the entity and its environment, including its internal control.

- **I**nquiries should be addressed to appropriate individuals, including the predecessor auditor.

- **A**nalytical procedures should be performed.

- **R**eview—other procedures should be performed.

- **C**lient representation letter should be obtained from management.

- **P**rofessional judgment should be used to evaluate results.

- **A**ccountant (CPA) should communicate results.

■ In addition to the standard review analysis of aggregated amounts, analytical procedures should be applied to disaggregated revenue data (by month, by product line, etc.).

■ The auditor is required to obtain evidence that interim data reconciles to accounting records.

■ In addition to the usual representations, the auditor should also obtain management's written representations related to internal controls and fraud.

3 Letters for Underwriters

"Comfort letters" are provided to an underwriter or other party (i.e., broker-dealer) just before the registration of the client's securities.

- The CPA is required to perform a review of interim financial information.

- The letter must include a restriction on its use (requesting party only).

- Negative assurance is provided for most financial information.

- Positive assurance is provided on the CPA's independence and compliance of financial statements with Securities Acts, assuming financial statements were audited; otherwise, negative assurance is provided.

Question 5   MCQ-09790

When issuing letters for underwriters, an accountant may provide positive assurance related to:

1. Unaudited financial statements that have been reviewed.

2. Compliance of management's discussion and analysis (MD&A) with SEC rules and regulations.

3. Compliance of the form of the audited financial statements with the requirements of the SEC Act.

4. Qualitative disclosures and market-sensitive instruments.

---

4 Comparison of SSARS and SAS Engagements

	Preparation Engagement	Compilation Engagement	Review Engagement			Audit Engagement
	SSARS	*SSARS*	*SSARS*	*SAS*	*PCAOB*	*SAS/PCAOB*
Level of Assurance	None	None	Limited			Reasonable.
Entities	Nonissuers only	Nonissuers only	Nonissuers	Nonissuers: Interim	Issuers: Interim	Nonissuers/Issuers
Knowledge Required	Knowledge of accounting principles and practices of industry; general understanding of client's business	Knowledge of accounting principles and practices of industry; general understanding of client's business	Same as compilation plus increased knowledge of client's business			Extensive knowledge of economy, industry, and client's business
Inquiry and Analytical Procedures Required	None unless information is questionable	None unless information is questionable	Inquiries of internal personnel Analytical procedures			Inquiries of external parties and internal personnel Analytical procedures Audit procedures
GAAP Disclosure Omitted	May omit, but need to disclose in the financial statement	May omit most without restricting use; warn with ending paragraph	All are required or modify review report			All required or "qualified/ adverse" opinion
GAAP Departures	May depart from GAAP, but need to disclose in the financial statement	Modify report to discuss GAAP departure	Modify report to discuss GAAP departure			Modify report "qualified/ adverse" opinion
Independence	Not required (non-attest engagement)	Not required but disclosure is required	Required			Required
Engagement Letter	Presumptively mandatory	Presumptively mandatory	Presumptively mandatory			Presumptively mandatory
Representation Letter	Not required	Not required	Required			Required
Understanding of Internal Control	Not required (no test work)	Not required (no test work)	Not required (no test work)	Required		Required
Errors and Irregularities Detection	Only obvious errors found when preparing financial statements	Only obvious errors found when reading financial statements	Only errors discovered through inquiry and analytical procedures			Must be designed to provide reasonable assurance of detection of material misstatements
Noncompliance with Laws and Regulations Detection	None, but known acts must be evaluated	None, but known acts must be evaluated	Only direct and material effect, that could be disclosed by inquiry and analytical procedures			Must be designed to reasonably assure detection of direct and material noncompliance with laws and regulations
FS Reported on (BS/IS/RE/CF)	One or more financial statements allowed to be prepared	One or more financial statements allowed to be reported on	One or more financial statements allowed if scope of inquiry and analytical procedures has not been restricted			One or more financial statements allowed if scope of audit is not limited and all necessary procedures are applied
Communication with Predecessor	Not required	Not required	Not required	Required		Required
Subsequent Event Inquiries	Not required	Not required	Required			Required

     Auditing Final Review

1 SSARS Review Report

- The review report provides limited assurance (less assurance than is provided by an audit) that no material modifications to the financial statements are required for conformity with GAAP (or other appropriate financial reporting framework).

- GAAP departures should be disclosed in a separate final paragraph in the review report titled "Known Departures from the [identify the applicable financial reporting framework]," or the accountant may withdraw from the engagement.

SSARS Review Report

Independent Accountant's Review Report

[*Appropriate addressee*]

We have reviewed the accompanying balance sheet of XYZ Company as of December 31, 20XX, and the related statements of income, retained earnings, and cash flows for the year then ended. A review includes primarily applying analytical procedures to management's financial data and making inquiries of company management. A review is substantially less in scope than an audit, the objective of which is the expression of an opinion regarding the financial statements as a whole. Accordingly, we do not express such an opinion.

Management's Responsibility for the Financial Statements

Management is responsible for the preparation and fair presentation of the financial statements in accordance with [*the applicable financial reporting framework (for example, accounting principles generally accepted in the United States of America)*]; and this includes the design, implementation, and maintenance of internal control relevant to the preparation and fair presentation of the financial statements that are free from material misstatement, whether due to fraud or error.

Accountant's Responsibility

Our responsibility is to conduct the review in accordance with Statements on Standards for Accounting and Review Services promulgated by the Accounting and Review Services Committee of the AICPA. Those standards require us to perform procedures to obtain limited assurance as a basis for reporting whether we are aware of material modifications that should be made to the financial statements for them to be in accordance with accounting principles generally accepted in the United States of America. We believe that the results of our procedures provide a reasonable basis for our report.

Accountant's Conclusion

Based on our review, **we are not aware of any material modifications** that should be made to the accompanying financial statements in order for them to be in accordance with [*the applicable financial reporting framework*].

[*Signature of accounting firm or accountant*]

[*Accountant's city and state*]

[*Date*]

Question 1

Financial statements of a nonissuer that have been reviewed by an accountant should be accompanied by a report stating that a review:

1. Provides only limited assurance that the financial statements are fairly presented.

2. Includes examining, on a test basis, information that is the representation of management.

3. Includes primarily applying analytical procedures to management's financial data and making inquiries of company management.

4. Does not contemplate obtaining corroborating audit evidence or applying certain other procedures ordinarily performed during an audit.

2 SSARS Compilation Report

SSARS Compilation Report

Management is responsible for the accompanying financial statements of XYZ Company, which comprise the balance sheets as of December 31, 20X2 and 20X1 and the related statements of income, changes in stockholders' equity, and cash flows for the years then ended, and the related notes to the financial statements in accordance with accounting principles generally accepted in the United States of America. We have performed compilation engagements in accordance with Statements on Standards for Accounting and Review Services promulgated by the Accounting and Review Services Committee of the AICPA. We did not audit or review the financial statements nor were we required to perform any procedures to verify the accuracy or completeness of the information provided by management. Accordingly, we do not express an opinion, a conclusion, nor provide any form of assurance on these financial statements.

[*Signature of accounting firm or accountant*]

[*Accountant's city and state*]

[*Date*]

- GAAP departures should be disclosed in a separate paragraph of the report, or the accountant may withdraw from the engagement.

- If substantially all required disclosures are omitted, the accountants report should clearly indicate this omission.

3 Comparative Reporting

Different services may be provided in different years.

- Increase in level of service—If a service upgrade (from compiled to reviewed) occurs:
  - The prior year report should be updated and issued as the last paragraph of the current period report.

- Decrease in level of service—If a service downgrade (from reviewed to compiled) occurs, three options exist:
  - Issue a compilation report and add a paragraph to the report describing the responsibility for the prior period statements. Include the date of original report, and a statement that no review procedures were performed after that date.
  - Issue two separate reports.
  - Issue a combined report presenting both full reports with an added statement to the review report indicating that no review procedures have since been performed.

- Decrease in level of service—If a service downgrade to a preparation engagement (from reviewed or compiled to preparation) occurs, there is no requirement to reference the prior period service performed.

4 Interim Review Report

- The auditor expresses limited assurance on interim financial information covering the period from the last audit to the date of the interim statements.

- GAAP departures must be disclosed.

- If the auditor determines that the disclosure related to substantial doubt about the entities' ability to continue as a going concern is inadequate, resulting in a departure from the applicable financial reporting framework, the auditor should modify the report.

- For issuers: As long as going concern disclosure is adequate, the auditor is not required to include an explanatory paragraph.

- For nonissuers: Add an emphasis-of-matter paragraph if management has included a statement that substantial doubt exists in its financial statements or (1) a going concern emphasis-of-matter paragraph was included in the prior year audit report, (2) the conditions of going concern still exist at interim, and (3) management's plans do not alleviate the substantial doubt.

- A lack of consistency paragraph is optional if there is adequate disclosure.

Independent Auditor's Review Report

[*Appropriate Addressee*]

Report on the Financial Statements

We have reviewed the accompanying [*describe the interim financial information or statements reviewed*] of ABC Company and subsidiaries as of September 30, 20X1, and for the three-month and nine-month periods then ended.

Management's Responsibility

The Company's management is responsible for the preparation and fair presentation of the interim financial information in accordance with [*identify the applicable financial reporting framework; for example, accounting principles generally accepted in the United States of America*]; this responsibility includes the design, implementation, and maintenance of internal control sufficient to provide a reasonable basis for the preparation and fair presentation of interim financial information in accordance with [*identify the applicable financial reporting framework; for example, accounting principles generally accepted in the United States of America*].

Auditor's Responsibility

Our responsibility is to conduct our review in accordance with auditing standards generally accepted in the United States of America applicable to reviews of interim financial information. A review of interim financial information consists principally of applying analytical procedures and making inquiries of persons responsible for financial and accounting matters. It is substantially less in scope than an audit conducted in accordance with auditing standards generally accepted in the United States, the objective of which is the expression of an opinion regarding the financial information. Accordingly, we do not express such an opinion.

Conclusion

Based on our review, we are not aware of any material modifications that should be made to the accompanying interim financial information for it to be in accordance with [*identify the applicable financial reporting framework; for example, accounting principles generally accepted in the United States of America*].

[*Auditor's Signature*]

[*Auditor's city and state*]

[*Date of the auditor's report*]

1 Other Information in Documents Containing Audited Financial Statements

The auditor must read the information and should try to resolve any material inconsistencies or material misstatements of fact directly with the client. The auditor may issue a disclaimer of opinion, or may be engaged to express an opinion on such information.

Question 1   MCQ-09774

In its annual report to shareholders, Walsh Co. included a letter to shareholders that contained financial summaries of the past two years. Walsh's auditor is expressing an unmodified opinion on Walsh's financial statements but has not been engaged to examine and report on this additional information. What is the auditor's responsibility concerning the financial summaries?

1. The auditor should express a qualified or adverse opinion because all financial statement information should be audited.

2. The auditor should include an emphasis-of-matter paragraph that includes a disclaimer of opinion on this information.

3. The auditor should inquire of management regarding the purpose of the supplementary information and the criteria used to prepare the information.

4. The auditor should read the letter to the shareholders and verify the information is materially consistent with the information presented in the audited financial statements.

---

2 Reporting on Supplementary Information in Relation to the Financial Statements as a Whole

An auditor may be engaged to report on supplementary information in relation to the financial statements as a whole.

2.1 Engagement Objectives

The auditor has two objectives in such engagements:

- to evaluate the presentation of the supplementary information in relation to the financial statements as a whole; and
- to report whether the supplementary information is fairly stated, in all material respects, in relation to the financial statements as a whole.

2.2 Auditor's Report

The auditor's report on the supplementary information may either be presented:

- in a separate report; or
- in the auditor's report on the financial statements as an other-matter paragraph (nonissuer) or as an additional paragraph (issuer).

3 Required Supplementary Information

Limited procedures should be performed. The auditor's report on the financial statements should include an other-matter paragraph related to the required supplementary information. An opinion is permitted but not required.

Question 2 · MCQ-09044

Jorge, CPA, has been asked to audit the financial statements of Capri Industries, which include supplementary information required by generally accepted accounting principles. Which best describes an appropriate response to this situation?

1. Jorge should not accept this engagement, since auditing information outside the basic financial statements goes beyond the scope of an audit.

2. Jorge may accept this engagement, but need not apply procedures specifically to the supplementary information, since it is outside the basic financial statements.

3. Jorge should not accept this engagement unless he is also hired to perform a separate attest engagement on the supplementary information.

4. Jorge may accept this engagement, but would need to perform certain procedures specifically with respect to the supplementary information.

4 Reports on Application of the Requirements of an Applicable Financial Reporting Framework

A reporting accountant may report on the application of the requirements of an applicable financial reporting framework to a specific transaction or the type of report that may be rendered on a specific entity's financial statements. The report should be restricted in use.

5 Reporting on Financial Statements Prepared in Accordance With a Financial Reporting Framework Generally Accepted in Another Country

A auditor practicing in the United States may be engaged to report on financial statements that have been prepared in accordance with a financial reporting framework generally accepted in another country that has not been adopted by a body designed by the AICPA to establish generally accepted accounting principles, when such audited financial statements are intended to be used outside the United States.

5.1   Distribution Outside the U.S. Only

Use either the other country's report, the report set out in the ISAs, or a U.S. form report that reflects that the financial statements being reported on have been prepared in accordance with a financial reporting framework generally accepted in another country.

5.2   Distribution Within the U.S.

Use the U.S. form report with an emphasis-of-matter paragraph that identifies the financial reporting framework, refers to the note in the financial statements that describes the framework, and indicates that the framework differs from accounting principles generally accepted in the United States of America.

Question 3   MCQ-09052

Which would most likely determine the appropriate form of audit report when financial statements are prepared in accordance with a financial reporting framework generally accepted in another country?

1. The other country's auditing standards.

2. The geographic location of the company.

3. The expected distribution of the financial statements.

4. The reciprocity agreement between that country and the United States.

1 Government Auditing—Standards and Supplementary Requirements

In performing an audit of government entities, the auditor may be responsible for meeting the requirements of as many as three sources of guidance:

- GAAS

- GAGAS (Generally Accepted Government Auditing Standards, also referred to as the Yellow Book)

- The Single Audit Act (2 CFR 200), which presents supplementary requirements only applicable if the entity spends federal financial assistance in excess of a specific amount.

2 GAAS Requirements for Compliance Audits

2.1 Objectives of Compliance Audits

- Obtain sufficient evidence to form an opinion on whether the entity complied, in all material respects, with the compliance requirements applicable to their programs.

- Report at the level specified in the governmental audit requirement.

- Identify audit and reporting requirements supplementary to GAAS and GAGAS and address those requirements (e.g., Single Audit Act requirements).

2.2 Overall Standards for Compliance Audits

- Perform a risk assessment (audit risk of noncompliance model)

- Design responses to the risk assessment

- Determine if supplementary audit requirements exist

- Obtain written representations from management

- Prepare reports

- Document risk and materiality

2.3   The Audit Risk of Noncompliance Model

The audit risk of noncompliance model adapts the terminology and relationships of the audit risk model. The risk of material noncompliance consists of inherent risk of noncompliance and control risk of noncompliance:

The Audit Risk of Noncompliance Model

Audit risk of noncompliance	=	Risk of material noncompliance (assessed by auditor)	×	Detection risk (controlled by auditor)

Risk of Material Noncompliance	Acceptable Level of Detection Risk	Determine "NET" of Testing
High ⬆ (Bad)	Low ⬇	High ⬆
Low ⬇ (Good)	High ⬆	Low ⬇

2.3.1   Inherent Risk of Noncompliance

The susceptibility of a compliance requirement to noncompliance that could be material assuming that there are no related controls.

■ Inherent risk exists independent of the audit.

■ The auditor cannot change this risk, but can change his/her assessment of the risk based on evidence gathered during the audit.

2.3.2   Control Risk of Noncompliance

The risk that noncompliance with a compliance requirement that could be material will not be prevented or detected on a timely basis by an entity's internal control over compliance.

■ Control risk exists independent of the audit.

■ The auditor cannot change this risk, but can change his/her assessment of the risk based on evidence gathered during the audit.

■ The stronger the system of controls over compliance, the greater the reliance that may be placed on those controls, and the fewer the tests of details (or the lower the quality) required.

2.3.3 Detection Risk of Noncompliance

The risk that the auditor will not detect noncompliance that exists and that undetected noncompliance could be material.

- Detection risk relates to the auditor's procedures.
- The auditor can change this risk by varying the nature, extent, or timing of audit procedures.
- As the acceptable level of detection risk decreases, the assurance provided from tests of details (including tests of implementation of corrective actions from previous audits) should increase.

2.4 Design Responses to Risk Assessment

- The auditor should design audit procedures, including tests of details of the entity's compliance with program requirements.
- The risk assessment, tests of controls, and analytical procedures are not sufficient to address the risk of material noncompliance. Tests of details must be performed.
- Tests of controls may be required if any one of the following conditions exist:
  - The risk assessment includes an expectation of the operating effectiveness of controls over compliance.
  - Substantive procedures do not provide enough evidence to support a conclusion.
  - Tests of controls are required by the applicable governmental audit requirements.

2.5 Determine if Supplementary Audit Requirements Exist

- The entity may have audit requirements that go beyond GAAS and GAGAS. The auditor must make that determination.
- A common example of supplementary audit requirements is the Single Audit requirements related to federal financial assistance described below.

2.6 Obtain a Written Management Representation Letter

Auditors must obtain a written management representation letter that includes statements that management:

- takes responsibility for compliance.
- takes responsibility for maintaining controls over compliance.
- asserts that they have disclosed all programs to the auditor.
- asserts that they have disclosed any known noncompliance or states that no such noncompliance exists.

2.7 Prepare Reports

The auditor may report in several ways, depending on the audit requirement. Possible reports include a(n):

- Opinion on compliance
- Report on internal control over compliance
- Combined report on compliance and internal control over compliance

2.8 Document Risk and Materiality

The auditor is responsible for documenting the following:

- The assessed risk of material noncompliance
- Responses to the risk assessment
- Materiality levels

3 Government Auditing Standards (GAGAS)

3.1 GAGAS: Source and Content Organization

- GAGAS are contained in the Government Auditing Standards, a publication of the Government Accountability Office (GAO) The publication is sometimes called the Yellow Book.
- Generally Accepted Government Auditing Standards (GAGAS) include ethical principles, general standards, standards for financial audits and attest engagements, and field work and reporting standards for performance audits.

3.2 Ethical Principles

The ethical principles that guide the work of auditors who conduct audits in accordance with GAGAS are:

- serving the public interest;
- integrity;
- objectivity;
- proper use of government information, resources, and positions; and
- professional behavior.

3.3 General Standards

The general standards provide guidance for performing financial audits, attestation engagements, and performance audits under GAGAS. The general standards include:

- independence (of mind and appearance);

- professional judgment;

- competence; and

- quality control and assurance (including maintenance of a quality control system and securing an external peer review at least once every three years).

3.4 Standards for Financial Audits: Additional GAGAS Requirements for Performing Financial Audits

- GAGAS describes a number of standards for financial audits in addition to the GAAS requirements.

- Additional standards include consideration of previous audits and attestation engagements, additional attention to fraud and noncompliance and abuse, development of findings to be reported to the entity and others, and audit documentation that provides evidence of supervision, supports findings, and describes the impact of departures from GAGAS.

3.5 Standards for Financial Audits: Additional GAGAS Requirements for Reporting on Financial Audits

- Auditors should include a statement in the auditor's report that they complied with GAGAS.

- Reporting should include a report on internal control over financial reporting and a report on compliance with provisions of laws, regulations, contracts or grant agreements that have a material effect on the financial statements.

- Auditors must report fraud and noncompliance with laws or regulations that have a material effect on the financial statements, noncompliance with provisions of contracts or grant agreements that have a material effect on the financial statements, and report abuse that is material either quantitatively or qualitatively.

- Auditors should report directly to outside parties when entity management fails to satisfy legal or regulatory requirements to report or when an entity's management fails to take time and appropriate steps to respond to known or likely fraud, noncompliance, or abuse.

- Auditors must report their findings and also solicit and report the views of responsible officials along with any planned corrective actions.

- GAGAS auditors should consider reducing materiality thresholds in response to public accountability issues, various legal and regulatory requirements, and the visibility and sensitivity of government programs.

- GAGAS auditors should consider reporting deficiencies early when the urgency or significance of findings requires faster corrective actions or follow-up or when ongoing noncompliance undetected by management should be stopped.

3.6 Reporting Standards and Requirements

3.6.1 Reporting on Compliance

When reporting on compliance under GAGAS, the report should include the following components:

- A statement that the audit complied with GAAS as well as GAGAS for financial audits.
- A report that states the auditor performed tests of compliance with provisions of laws, regulations, contracts, and grant agreements.
- Identification of noncompliance issues discovered during the audit.

3.6.2 Reporting on Internal Control

When reporting on internal control under GAGAS, the report should include the following components:

- A statement that the audit complied with GAAS as well as GAGAS for financial audits.
- The auditor asserts that internal control over financial reporting was considered as part of planning and performing the audit of the financial statements, but not for the purpose of expressing an opinion on internal control. The internal control reporting requirement under GAGAS differs from the objective of an audit of internal control (as part of an integrated audit).

  (*Note:* An integrated audit is not required for nonissuers under SAS. A nonissuer may engage an auditor to perform a financial statement audit only. In a financial statement audit only under SAS, an auditor will report on internal control only if deficiencies are discovered during the financial statement audit.)

  - An audit of internal control (as part of an integrated audit) requires the auditor to provide a high level of assurance about internal control over financial reporting in the form of an opinion.
  - GAGAS does not require the auditor to render an opinion on the effectiveness of internal control over financial reporting. However, the auditor is not precluded from rendering an opinion on internal control if sufficient procedures have been performed.

- A statement that no opinion is expressed on internal control.
- The definition of deficiency in internal control and material weakness in internal control.
- A description of identified material weakness and significant deficiencies in internal control.
- A statement that no material weaknesses were found if none were found.

3.6.3 Reporting Noncompliance

Material instances of noncompliance should be reported in a separate communication to the entity and should be noted in the auditor's report.

- Material instances are defined as:
  - failure to follow requirements; or
  - violations of rules contained in statutes, regulations, contracts, or grants.
- Reporting illegal acts is required.

Question 1   MCQ-08825

Reporting standards associated with government audits include requirements in addition to those associated with generally accepted auditing standards. A requirement that distinguishes audits performed in accordance with government auditing standards from audits that are not subject to these standards is:

1. An opinion on the financial statements taken as a whole.
2. A written communication of the auditor's work on internal control.
3. An opinion on internal control over financial reporting.
4. No opinion on the financial statements is required.

---

4 Single Audit Act (2 CFR 200) Requirements

4.1 Criteria

- The Single Audit Act applies to entities that receive and spend total financial awards equal to or in excess of $750,000 in a fiscal year.

- The Single Audit Act allows for either a single audit that covers the entire entity, or program specific audits associated with an individual award. Program-specific audits are only available to grant recipients who only have one federal program and who are not required to have a financial statement audit.

4.2 Materiality Determinations

- Materiality of a transaction or other compliance finding is considered separately in relation to each major program, not just in relation to the financial statement as a whole.

- Programs classified as major are generally those that expend $750,000 or more in federal financial assistance. Smaller programs may be classified as major if they are deemed to be high risk.

Question 2   MCQ-09027

The requirements to perform a Single Audit under the provisions of 2 CFR 200 apply to entities that:

1. Receive $500,000 in federal financial assistance in a fiscal year.
2. Receive $750,000 in federal financial assistance in a fiscal year.
3. Receive and expend $500,000 in federal financial assistance in a fiscal year.
4. Receive and expend $750,000 in federal financial assistance in fiscal year.

---

5 GAAS, GAGAS, and SAA: Comparison of Reports

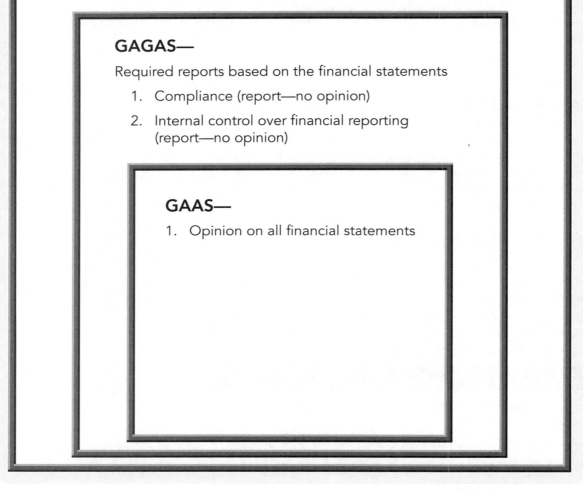

Single Audit Act (2 CFR 200)—

Required reports based on federal programs

1. Compliance (opinion)
2. Internal control over compliance applicable to each major program (report—no opinion)
3. Schedule of findings and questioned costs

GAGAS—

Required reports based on the financial statements

1. Compliance (report—no opinion)
2. Internal control over financial reporting (report—no opinion)

GAAS—

1. Opinion on all financial statements

Question 3

MCQ-04636

A government audit may extend beyond an examination leading to the expression of an opinion on the fairness of financial presentation to include:

	Program Results	Compliance	Economy & Efficiency
1.	Yes	Yes	No
2.	Yes	Yes	Yes
3.	No	Yes	Yes
4.	Yes	No	Yes

1 Special Purpose Frameworks

1.1 Types of Special Purpose Frameworks

Special purpose frameworks include:

- Cash basis.

- Income tax basis.

- Basis required by regulatory agency.

- Basis required by contract.

- Any other basis of accounting that uses a definite set of logical, reasonable criteria that is applied to all material items appearing in the financial statements.

1.2 Report on Special Purpose Frameworks

1.2.1 Report Elements

- Use non-GAAP titles for financial statements.

- Add an emphasis-of-matter paragraph that indicates that the financial statements are prepared using a special purpose framework, states that the basis of presentation is different than GAAP, and refers the reader to the related footnote.

- Add an other-matter paragraph that restricts the use of the report if the financial statements are prepared using a contractual or regulatory basis, or another basis of accounting that uses a definite set of logical, reasonable criteria, unless the financial statements are regulatory basis financial statements intended for general use.

- If the special purpose financial statements are prepared in accordance with a regulatory basis and intended for general use, the auditor should express an opinion about whether the financial statements are:

  - fairly presented, in all material respects, in accordance with GAAP.

  - prepared in accordance with the special purpose framework.

1.2.2 Sample Auditor's Report on Financial Statements Prepared in Accordance With a Special Purpose Framework (Cash Basis)

Independent Auditor's Report

[*Appropriate Addressee*]

We have audited the accompanying financial statements of ABC Partnership, which comprise the statement of assets and liabilities arising from cash transactions as of December 31, 20X1, and the related statement of revenue collected and expenses paid for the year then ended, and the related notes to the financial statements.

Management's Responsibility for the Financial Statements

Management is responsible for the preparation and fair presentation of these financial statements in accordance with the cash basis of accounting described in Note X; this includes determining that the cash basis of accounting is an acceptable basis for the preparation of the financial statements in the circumstances. Management is also responsible for the design, implementation, and maintenance of internal control relevant to the preparation and fair presentation of financial statements that are free from material misstatement, whether due to fraud or error.

Auditor's Responsibility

Our responsibility is to express an opinion on the financial statements based on our audit. We conducted our audit in accordance with auditing standards generally accepted in the United States of America. Those standards require that we plan and perform the audit to obtain reasonable assurance about whether the financial statements are free from material misstatement.

An audit involves performing procedures to obtain audit evidence about the amounts and disclosures in the financial statements. The procedures selected depend on the auditor's judgment, including the assessment of the risks of material misstatement of the financial statements, whether due to fraud or error. In making those risk assessments, the auditor considers internal control relevant to the partnership's preparation and fair presentation of the financial statements in order to design audit procedures that are appropriate in the circumstances, but not for the purpose of expressing an opinion on the effectiveness of the partnership's internal control. Accordingly, we express no such opinion. An audit also includes evaluating the appropriateness of accounting policies used and the reasonableness of significant accounting estimates made by management, as well as evaluating the overall presentation of the financial statements.

We believe that the audit evidence we have obtained is sufficient and appropriate to provide a basis for our opinion.

Opinion

In our opinion, the financial statements referred to above present fairly, in all material respects, the assets and liabilities arising from cash transactions of ABC Partnership as of December 31, 20X1, and its revenues collected and expenses paid during the year then ended in accordance with the cash basis of accounting described in Note X.

Basis of Accounting

We draw attention to Note X of the financial statements, which describes the basis of accounting. The financial statements are prepared on the cash basis of accounting, which is a basis of accounting other than accounting principles generally accepted in the United States of America. Our opinion is not modified with respect to this matter.

[*Auditor's signature*]

[*Auditor's city and state*]

[*Date of the auditor's report*]

2 Single Financial Statements and Specified Elements, Accounts, or Items

An audit of a single financial statement or of specific elements, accounts, or items of a financial statement may be performed as a separate engagement or in conjunction with an audit of an entity's complete set of financial statements. An incomplete presentation that is otherwise in accordance with GAAP is a type of single financial statement.

2.1 Audit Procedures

The auditor should perform procedures on any interrelated items, such as sales and receivables or inventory and cost of goods sold.

2.1.1 Stockholders' Equity

When the specific element is, or is based on, stockholders' equity, the auditor should perform procedures necessary to express an opinion about financial position.

2.1.2 Net Income

When the specific element is, or is based on, net income or the equivalent, the auditor should perform procedures necessary to express an opinion about financial position and results of operations.

2.2 Modified Opinion on the Complete Set of Financial Statements

If the auditor issues a modified opinion on the complete set of financial statements that is relevant to the audit of a specific element, the auditor should:

▪ Express an adverse opinion on the specific element when the modified opinion on the complete set of financial statements is due to a material misstatement.

▪ Express a disclaimer of opinion on the specific element when the modified opinion on the complete set of financial statements is due to a scope limitation.

2.3 Adverse or Disclaimer of Opinion on the Complete Set of Financial Statements

When the auditor expresses an adverse opinion or a disclaimer of opinion on the complete set of financial statements, an unmodified opinion on a specific element in the same auditor's report would contradict the adverse opinion or disclaimer of opinion and would be the same as expressing a piecemeal opinion.

- In this situation, when the auditor considers it appropriate to express an unmodified opinion on the specific element, the auditor should do so only if:
  - the opinion on the specific element is not published with and does not accompany the auditor's report on the complete set of financial statements; and
- the specific element does not constitute a major portion of the entity's complete set of financial statement or the specific element is not, or is not based on, stockholders' equity or net income.
  - A single financial statement is considered to be a major portion of a complete set of financial statements.

2.4 Auditor's Report on a Single Financial Statement

Independent Auditor's Report

[*Appropriate Addressee*]

We have audited the accompanying balance sheet of ABC Company as of December 31, 20X1, and the related notes to the financial statement.

Management's Responsibility for the Financial Statement

Management is responsible for the preparation and fair presentation of this financial statement in accordance with accounting principles generally accepted in the United States of America; this includes the design, implementation, and maintenance of internal control relevant to the preparation and fair presentation of the financial statement that is free from material misstatement, whether due to fraud or error.

Auditor's Responsibility

Our responsibility is to express an opinion on the financial statement based on our audit. We conducted our audit in accordance with auditing standards generally accepted in the United States of America. Those standards require that we plan and perform the audit to obtain reasonable assurance about whether the financial statement is free from material misstatement.

An audit involves performing procedures to obtain audit evidence about the amounts and disclosures in the financial statement. The procedures selected depend on the auditor's judgment, including the assessment of the risks of material misstatement of the financial statement, whether due to fraud or error. In making those risk assessments, the auditor considers internal control relevant to the entity's preparation and fair presentation of the financial statement in order to design audit procedures that are appropriate in the circumstances, but not for the purpose of expressing an opinion on the effectiveness of the entity's internal control. Accordingly, we express no such opinion. An audit also includes evaluating the appropriateness of accounting policies used and the reasonableness of significant accounting estimates made by management, as well as evaluating the overall presentation of the financial statement.

We believe that the audit evidence we have obtained is sufficient and appropriate to provide a basis for our opinion.

Opinion

In our opinion, the financial statement referred to above presents fairly, in all material respects, the financial position of ABC Company as of December 31, 20X1 in accordance with accounting principles generally accepted in the United States of America.

[*Auditor's signature*]
[*Auditor's city and state*]
[*Date of the auditor's report*]

2.5   Auditor's Report on a Specific Element

Independent Auditor's Report

[*Appropriate Addressee*]

We have audited the accompanying schedule of accounts receivable of ABC Company as of December 31, 20X1, and the related notes to the schedule.

Management's Responsibility for the Schedule

Management is responsible for the preparation and fair presentation of this schedule in accordance with accounting principles generally accepted in the United States of America; this includes the design, implementation, and maintenance of internal control relevant to the preparation and fair presentation of the schedule that is free from material misstatement, whether due to fraud or error.

Auditor's Responsibility

Our responsibility is to express an opinion on the schedule based on our audit. We conducted our audit in accordance with auditing standards generally accepted in the United States of America. Those standards require that we plan and perform the audit to obtain reasonable assurance about whether the schedule is free from material misstatement.

An audit involves performing procedures to obtain audit evidence about the amounts and disclosures in the schedule. The procedures selected depend on the auditor's judgment, including the assessment of the risks of material misstatement of the schedule, whether due to fraud or error. In making those risk assessments, the auditor considers internal control relevant to the entity's preparation and fair presentation of the schedule in order to design audit procedures that are appropriate in the circumstances, but not for the purpose of expressing an opinion on the effectiveness of the entity's internal control. Accordingly, we express no such opinion. An audit also includes evaluating the appropriateness of accounting policies used and the reasonableness of significant accounting estimates made by management, as well as evaluating the overall presentation of the schedule.

We believe that the audit evidence we have obtained is sufficient and appropriate to provide a basis for our opinion.

Opinion

In our opinion, the schedule referred to above presents fairly, in all material respects, the accounts receivable of ABC Company as of December 31, 20X1 in accordance with accounting principles generally accepted in the United States of America.

Other Matter

We have audited, in accordance with auditing standards generally accepted in the United States of America, the financial statements of ABC Company as of and for the year ended December 31, 20X1, and our report thereon, dated March 15, 20X2, expressed an unmodified opinion on those financial statements.

[*Auditor's signature*]

[*Auditor's city and state*]

[*Date of the auditor's report*]

Question 2

An auditor is engaged by the client to report on inventory and the complete set of financial statements. The auditor expresses a qualified opinion on the complete set of financial statements due to a material misstatement of inventory and cost of goods sold. Under these circumstances, the CPA should express:

1. A qualified opinion on inventory.
2. An adverse opinion on inventory.
3. A disclaimer of opinion on inventory.
4. An unmodified opinion on inventory in a report that does not accompany the auditor's report on the complete set of financial statements.

Question 3

Which of the following is *true* about a report on a specific element of a financial statement?

1. An audit of the complete financial statements is required.
2. An unmodified opinion may not be expressed if an adverse opinion or disclaimer of opinion was expressed on the complete financial statements.
3. There should be a reference to both GAAS and GAAP in the report.
4. A restrictive use paragraph is required.

3 Compliance With Contractual or Regulatory Requirements Related to Audited Financial Statements

3.1 Negative Assurance

The auditor issues negative assurance on compliance in the form of a statement that nothing came to the auditor's attention that caused the auditor to believe that the entity failed to comply with the specified aspects of the contractual agreement or regulatory requirement.

3.2 Report on Compliance

The report on compliance should be in writing and may either be a separate report or provided in one or more paragraphs in the auditor's report on the financial statements.

3.2.1 Separate Report on Compliance

Independent Auditor's Report

[*Appropriate Addressee*]

We have audited, in accordance with auditing standards generally accepted in the United States of America, the financial statements of XYZ Company, which comprise the balance sheet as of December 31, 20X2, and the related statements of income, changes in stockholders' equity, and cash flows for the year then ended, and the related notes to the financial statements, and have issued our report thereon dated February 16, 20X3.

In connection with our audit, nothing came to our attention that caused us to believe that XYZ Company failed to comply with the terms, covenants, provisions, or conditions of sections XX to YY inclusive, of the Indenture dated July 21, 20X0, with ABC Bank, insofar as they relate to accounting matters. However, our audit was not directed primarily toward obtaining knowledge of such noncompliance. Accordingly, had we performed additional procedures, other matters may have come to our attention regarding the Company's noncompliance with the above-referenced terms, covenants, provisions, or conditions of the Indenture, insofar as they relate to accounting matters.

This report is intended solely for the information and use of the boards of directors and management of XYZ Company and ABC Bank and is not intended to be and should not be used by anyone other than these specified parties.

[*Auditor's signature*]

[*Auditor's city and state*]

[*Date of the auditor's report*]

Question 4 — MCQ-09782

Which of the following reports requires restricted use language in the report?

1. A report on financial statements prepared on the tax basis of accounting.

2. A report on a client's compliance with a contractual agreement, assuming the report is prepared in connection with a financial statement audit of the complete financial statements.

3. A report on the balance sheet only.

4. A report on an examination of a financial forecast.

Class Question Explanations

Topic A

QUESTION 1

Choice "4" is correct.

Intentional manipulation of accounting records indicates that management lacks integrity, and as a result, the auditor most likely would conclude that a financial statement audit cannot be performed.

Choice "1" is incorrect. The auditor can accept the engagement even if the auditor does not have experience in the particular industry. However, the auditor should obtain an understanding of the client's business and industry (e.g., by reading appropriate publications) after acceptance of the engagement.

Choice "2" is incorrect. A restriction imposed by circumstances beyond the control of management, such as a hurricane, does not prevent an auditor from accepting an engagement. Additionally, the auditor may be able to perform alternative procedures.

Choice "3" is incorrect. A management-imposed restriction that the auditor believes will result in a qualified opinion does not prevent an auditor from accepting an engagement. However, if the auditor believed the management imposed scope limitation would result in a disclaimer of opinion, then the auditor might conclude that a financial statement audit cannot be performed.

Topic B

QUESTION 1

Choice "3" is correct.

A successor auditor's inquiries of the predecessor auditor should include questions regarding communications to management and those charged with governance regarding significant deficiencies (and material weaknesses) in internal control.

Choice "1" is incorrect. The successor auditor generally would not inquire about the number of personnel assigned to the predecessor's engagement.

Choice "2" is incorrect. The successor auditor is responsible for making his or her own judgments regarding the audit, and would not typically inquire regarding the predecessor auditor's judgments with respect to the internal audit function.

Choice "4" is incorrect. The successor auditor generally would not specifically inquire about the response rate for confirmations of accounts receivable. However, the successor auditor would be able to obtain this information when reviewing the predecessor's workpapers.

Auditing I

Topic C

QUESTION 1   MCQ-09799

Choice "2" is correct.

The engagement letter should include a statement regarding the inherent limitations of the audit. This inherent limitation statement describes the unavoidable risk that some material misstatements may not be detected, even though the audit is properly planned and performed in accordance with GAAS.

Choice "1" is incorrect. The engagement letter generally would not describe the advantages of statistical sampling.

Choice "3" is incorrect. An auditor may not be paid in stock of the entity because this would impair the auditor's independence.

Choice "4" is incorrect. The assessment of risk of material misstatement is not included in the engagement letter. The risk of material misstatement is part of the planning process that occurs after engagement acceptance.

Topic D

QUESTION 1   MCQ-09811

Choice "4" is correct.

According to PCAOB standards, audit documentation must be retained for seven years.

Choices "1", "2", and "3" are incorrect, per the above explanation.

QUESTION 2   MCQ-09844

Choice "3" is correct.

Audit documentation should show who performed the work and the date the work was completed.

Choice "1" is incorrect. Audit documentation should be prepared in enough detail so that an experienced auditor, not necessarily a new staff auditor, who has no previous connection with the audit can understand the conclusions reached and any significant judgments made to reach those conclusions.

Choice "2" is incorrect. Audit documentation should enable quality performance reviews and inspections to be performed on the specific audit but does not necessarily by itself "monitor" the effectiveness of the CPA firm's quality control activities. Monitoring is performed at the firm level, not at the individual audit engagement level.

Choice "4" is incorrect. The auditor's understanding of internal control can be documented in a variety of different ways. There is no requirement in professional standards that the design and implementation of internal control must include a flowchart depicting the internal control process.

Topic E

QUESTION 1

Choice "2" is correct.

The communication must include material misstatements discovered, even if corrected by management.

Choice "1" is incorrect because while communication to management is allowed, it is not required.

Choice "3" is incorrect because disagreements with management, as well as the other required disclosures, should be communicated in writing when in the auditor's professional judgment, oral communication would be inadequate. Therefore, oral communication of such matters is not entirely precluded.

Choice "4" is incorrect because frequently recurring immaterial misstatements may be communicated if they indicate a particular bias in the preparation of the financial statement.

QUESTION 2

Choice "1" is correct.

The auditor must describe his or her responsibility under generally accepted auditing standards in the communication to those charged with governance, but this description is not included in the management representation letter. The representation letter (and not the communication to those charged with governance) would include management's responsibility for fair presentation of the financial statements in conformity with generally accepted accounting principles. Both communications should include uncorrected, nontrivial misstatements identified by the auditor.

Choices "2", "3", and "4" are incorrect, based on the above explanation.

Topic F

QUESTION 1

Choice "2" is correct.

Significant deficiencies and material weaknesses must be communicated in writing to management and those charged with governance. The auditor is required to define and separately identify significant deficiencies and material weaknesses.

Choice "1" is incorrect. Significant deficiencies and material weaknesses must be communicated in writing to management and those charged with governance.

Choice "3" is incorrect. The auditor is not required to obtain a management response to significant deficiencies or material weaknesses.

Choice "4" is incorrect. The auditor is required to define and separately identify significant deficiencies and material weaknesses.

Auditing I

Topic G

QUESTION 1   MCQ-09616

Choice "3" is correct.

Independence is impaired when a close family member of a covered person is employed by the client in an accounting or financial reporting role. Employment in the customer service department is not an accounting or financial reporting role and therefore the wife's employment at Warehouse Company would not impair independence.

Choice "1" is incorrect. Independence is impaired if any covered person, including the lead partner, serves on the client's board of directors.

Choice "2" is incorrect. Independence is impaired if the accounting firm employs a former employee of the audit client and the individual participates in an audit related to the period in which the individual was employed by the client. In this case, the former controller worked for Warehouse during Year 10 and therefore should not participate in the audit of Warehouse's Year 10 financial statements.

Choice "4" is incorrect. Independence is impaired when a former member of the audit engagement team is employed by an issuer client in a financial oversight role during the one-year preceding the commencement of audit procedures. In this case, Smith and Company cannot audit Warehouse's Year 10 financial statements because the former engagement manager was employed by Warehouse as the CFO during Year 10.

QUESTION 2   MCQ-09477

Choice "3" is correct.

Under the Independence Rule of the Code of Conduct, independence is impaired if there is a direct financial interest in an audit client regardless of materiality.

Choices "1", "2", and "4" are incorrect because materiality would be important in considering their effects.

QUESTION 3   MCQ-09589

Choice "2" is correct.

The Sarbanes-Oxley Act of 2002 requires registered firms to maintain audit documentation for seven years, not five years.

Choice "1" is incorrect. The Sarbanes-Oxley Act prohibits auditors from performing certain non-audit services, including internal control outsourcing, for audit clients who are issuers.

Choice "3" is incorrect. The Sarbanes-Oxley Act requires the lead and reviewing partners to rotate off the audit engagement after five years.

Choice "4" is incorrect. The Sarbanes-Oxley Act requires the preapproval of tax services to be provided to audit clients.

QUESTION 4

Choice "1" is correct.

Under Department of Labor (DOL) rules, independence is not impaired when an actuary associated with the audit firm provides services to the benefit plan.

Choice "2" is incorrect. Under DOL rules, auditor independence is impaired by direct or material indirect interests in the benefit plan or the plan sponsor.

Choice "3" is incorrect. Under DOL rules, independence is impaired if a member of the audit firm maintains the financial records of the benefit plan.

Choice "4" is incorrect. Under DOL rules, independence is impaired if a member of the engagement team serves on the board of directors of the plan sponsor.

Topic H

QUESTION 1

Choice "2" is correct.

A system of quality control should include human resource policies and practices, such as recruitment and hiring, determining capabilities and competencies, assigning personnel to engagements, professional development, and performance evaluation, compensation and advancement.

Choice "1" is incorrect. A CPA firm is required to adopt a system of quality control for its auditing, attestation, and accounting and review services.

Choice "3" is incorrect. A system of quality control should be designed, implemented, and maintained to improve the overall conduct of the firm's professional practice; however, this does not necessarily improve audit efficiency.

Choice "4" is incorrect. While an effective system of quality control is conducive to complying with generally accepted auditing standards, it does not necessarily ensure that such standards are followed on every individual audit engagement.

Auditing Final Review

Topic A

QUESTION 1   MCQ-09804

Choice "3" is correct.

Performing inquiries of outside legal counsel regarding pending litigation would not be performed during the planning stage.

Choice "1" is incorrect. Audit planning includes determining the timing of testing.

Choice "2" is incorrect. During the planning stage, the auditor engages in several information gathering activities to obtain knowledge of the client's business, which may include touring the client's facilities.

Choice "4" is incorrect. During the planning stage, the auditor will determine the effect of information technology on the audit because this will help determine the extent of testing.

QUESTION 2   MCQ-09072

Choice "2" is correct.

In an audit conducted in accordance with GAAS, the auditor must document the audit plan, setting forth in detail the procedures necessary to complete the engagement's objectives.

Choices "1" and "4" are incorrect. Documentation of the auditor's understanding of the client's internal control is required, but may take different forms: a narrative, an internal control questionnaire, a flowchart, or simply a memorandum (for a small client) may be sufficient.

Choice "3" is incorrect. A planning memo, while recommended, is not required under GAAS.

Topic B

QUESTION 1   MCQ-09071

Choice "2" is correct.

A lack of physical controls over the safeguarding of assets implies that internal controls are inadequate. Inherent limitations do not relate to controls that are missing or nonexistent, but rather to reasons why internal controls cannot provide absolute assurance.

Choice "1" is incorrect. A programming error in the design of an automated control is a human error. The fact that we cannot completely eliminate human error is one of the inherent limitations of internal control.

Choice "3" is incorrect. Management override of internal control is an inherent limitation of internal control.

Choice "4" is incorrect. Deliberate circumvention of controls by collusion among two or more people is an inherent limitation of internal control.

Auditing Final Review

Auditing II

QUESTION 2

MCQ-09054

Choice "1" is correct.

While obtaining an understanding of internal control, the auditor is required to obtain an understanding of the design of controls and determine whether they have been implemented. The auditor is not required to evaluate the operating effectiveness of controls, but may choose to do so if it is efficient.

Choice "2" is incorrect. The auditor is not required to evaluate the operating effectiveness of controls while obtaining an understanding of internal control.

Choice "3" is incorrect. The auditor may choose to evaluate the operating effectiveness of controls while obtaining an understanding of internal control, if it is efficient to do so.

Choice "4" is incorrect. While obtaining an understanding of internal control, the auditor is required to obtain an understanding of the design of controls and determine whether they have been implemented.

QUESTION 3

MCQ-08111

Choice "1" is correct.

There are two types of reports on the processing of transactions by service organizations: "reports on controls placed in operation" and "reports on controls placed in operation and tests of operating effectiveness." The former do not include tests of operating effectiveness and, therefore, are not intended to provide the user auditor with a basis for reducing the assessment of control risk below the maximum. Accordingly, such reports should include a disclaimer of opinion regarding the operating effectiveness of the controls.

Choice "2" is incorrect because the report should contain an indication that the controls were suitably designed to achieve specified control objectives, but it does not provide any assurance regarding the achievement of the user organization's (in this case, the retailer's) objectives.

Choice "3" is incorrect because the service auditor (Cook) is not required to identify the service organization's (i.e., PDC's) controls relevant to specific financial statement assertions, because this is not a financial statement audit.

Choice "4" is incorrect because the service auditor (Cook) is not required to disclose the assessed level of control risk for the service organization (PDC).

QUESTION 4

MCQ-04383

Choice "3" is correct.

Test data allows the auditor to determine whether adequate controls exist over data processing. Test data consists of fictitious entries or inputs that are processed through the client's computer system under the control of the auditor. The client's computerized payroll system should have adequate controls to prevent input of invalid employee I.D. numbers.

Choices "1", "2", and "4" are incorrect because these controls do not involve the client's computer system and therefore cannot be tested using test data.

Auditing II

QUESTION 5

Choice "2" is correct.

Test data consists of "dummy" data run through the client's computer system. The data should be processed under the auditor's control.

Choice "1" is incorrect because only transactions that the auditor wishes to test must be used.

Choice "3" is incorrect because while the auditor will frequently use many valid and invalid conditions, it is not feasible to test every possible valid and invalid condition using a test data approach.

Choice "4" is incorrect because the objective of the test data approach is to test programs that the client uses to process data. Using different programs defeats the primary purpose of the test.

Topic C

QUESTION 1

Choice "3" is correct.

The auditor must obtain reasonable assurance about whether the financial statements are free of material misstatements, whether caused by error or fraud.

Choices "1", "2", and "4" are incorrect, based on the above explanation.

QUESTION 2

Choice "2" is correct.

Although the risk of material misstatement due to fraud may be greatest when all three fraud risk factors are observed, the inability to observe any or all of these conditions does not imply that there is no fraud risk.

Choice "1" is incorrect. Fraud risk factors include incentives/pressures, opportunity, and rationalization.

Choice "3" is incorrect. Although the risk of material misstatement due to fraud may be greatest when all three fraud risk factors are observed, the existence of all three risk factors is not an absolute indication of fraud.

Choice "4" is incorrect. It is true that fraud risk factors are often present in circumstances where fraud has occurred.

QUESTION 3

Choice "1" is correct.

The auditor provides reasonable, not absolute, assurance that the material misstatements are free from error, whether due to error or fraud.

Choice "2", "3", and "4" are all required documentation regarding the required fraud brainstorming session.

Auditing II

Topic D

Choice "1" is correct.

The auditor would initially have planned the audit to achieve a low level of audit risk. If the risk of material misstatement increased, the auditor would need to reduce detection risk to achieve the same low level of audit risk as initially planned.

Choice "2" is incorrect. The increase in the risk of material misstatement results in an increase in overall audit risk. Increasing detection risk would only exacerbate this problem by increasing audit risk even further.

Choice "3" is incorrect. If the auditor does not modify the desired level of detection risk, it is true that the overall level of audit risk will increase, but this is not the most likely situation. An auditor who discovers a higher risk than initially anticipated would need to develop an appropriate response to offset this increase in risk, so that an overall low level of audit risk could still be attained.

Choice "4" is incorrect. Assuming that the auditor had already planned the audit to achieve an appropriately low level of audit risk, the auditor would most likely revise audit procedures in an attempt to achieve the same low level of audit risk as initially planned. Although it is possible that the auditor would reduce detection risk enough to actually lower overall audit risk, this is not the most likely response to the scenario described.

Choice "4" is correct.

As the acceptable level of detection risk increases, the assurance that must be provided by substantive tests can decrease. Therefore, the auditor may reduce the sample size.

Choice "1" is incorrect. As the acceptable level of detection risk increases, the level of assurance required from substantive tests decreases. Changing the nature of substantive tests from a less effective to a more effective procedure provides more assurance and is more likely to result from a decrease (not increase) in detection risk.

Choice "2" is incorrect. As the acceptable level of detection risk increases, the assurance that must be provided by substantive tests can decrease. Changing the timing of substantive tests from interim to year-end provides more assurance and is more likely to result from a decrease (not increase) in detection risk.

Choice "3" is incorrect. Although inherent risk affects the level of detection risk, detection risk does not affect the level of inherent risk. Inherent risk exists independently of the audit.

Choice "3" is correct.

Analytical procedures used in planning the audit should focus on enhancing the auditor's understanding of the client's business and the transactions and events that have occurred since the last audit date.

Choice "1" is incorrect. Analytical procedures used in planning do not reduce tests of controls or substantive tests.

Choice "2" is incorrect. Analytical procedures used in planning are not designed to identify material misstatements.

Choice "4" is incorrect. Audit evidence has not yet been gathered during the planning process, so its adequacy cannot be assessed.

QUESTION 4

Choice "3" is correct.

The required risk assessment discussion should include consideration of the risk of management override of controls.

Choice "1" is incorrect. The discussion about the susceptibility of the entity's financial statements to material misstatement may be held concurrently from the discussion about the susceptibility of the entity's financial statements to fraud.

Choice "2" is incorrect. The discussion must involve all "key" members who participate on the audit team, including the engagement partner.

Choice "4" is incorrect. The risk assessment discussion is required to occur at the start of the audit, during the planning phase.

Topic E

QUESTION 1

Choice "2" is correct.

The occurrence assertion addresses whether recorded entries are valid. The direction of this test is from the recorded entry in the voucher register to the supporting documents.

Choice "1" is incorrect. Completeness addresses whether all transactions and events are included, and would involve tracing from support for purchases to the recorded entry.

Choices "3" and "4" are incorrect. Tracing from the voucher register to supporting documents provides only limited evidence about allocation and valuation, or about rights and obligations.

QUESTION 2

Choice "1" is correct.

Tracing from source documents (evidence of shipments) to the accounting records (sales journal) provides evidence of completeness. If the auditor finds a shipment that was not recorded, this would indicate a lack of completeness of sales.

Choice "2" is incorrect. Accounts receivable turnover may vary from year to year based on changes in the level of credit sales and receivables. With more than one factor affecting this ratio, however, it is not the most likely means of detecting an understatement in sales.

Choice "3" is incorrect. Using common size analysis, total revenue is set at 100 percent for each company. Comparison of common size financial statements would not be useful in trying to identify understatements in credit sales.

Choice "4" is incorrect. If an audit test starts with a selection of *recorded* sales, unrecorded sales will not be discovered by this test.

Auditing II

QUESTION 3

Choice "2" is correct.

The auditor is not required to evaluate operating effectiveness as part of understanding internal control, and therefore, need not document the basis for this decision.

Choice "1" is incorrect. A written audit plan setting forth the procedures necessary to accomplish the audit objectives is required to be documented.

Choice "3" is incorrect. An auditor should document key elements of the understanding of the entity and its environment, including each of the five components of internal control. The five components include the entity's control activities.

Choice "4" is incorrect. The assessment of the risks of material misstatement at both the financial statement and relevant assertion levels are required to be documented.

Topic F

QUESTION 1

Choice "4" is correct.

An increase in level of supervision represents an appropriate overall response to an increase in financial statement level risk.

Choice "1" is incorrect. An appropriate overall response to an increase in financial statement level risk is to incorporate a greater level of unpredictability into the audit. Informing management of the specific details of substantive procedures would make the audit more predictable.

Choice "2" is incorrect. Testing of controls in a financial statement audit is performed when the auditor's risk assessment is based on the assumption that the controls are operating effectively or when substantive procedures alone are insufficient.

Choice "3" is incorrect. An auditor most likely would perform tests at period end, rather than interim, because it provides greater assurance.

QUESTION 2

Choice "4" is correct.

Using a combined approach involves identifying specific internal controls relevant to specific assertions that are likely to prevent or detect material misstatements in those assertions. If those controls are found to be operating effectively, substantive testing can be reduced.

Choice "1" is incorrect. Using a combined approach would most likely lead to less extensive substantive tests with smaller sample sizes.

Choice "2" is incorrect. A combined approach is based on the relationship between the operating effectiveness of controls and the required level of substantive testing. The level of inherent risk is not part of this evaluation.

Choice "3" is incorrect. Substantive tests performed at year-end would be more consistent with a substantive approach, which would require more competent substantive testing to be performed.

Topic G

QUESTION 1

Choice "3" is correct.

The client's release of quarterly results before the SEC-prescribed deadline would not result in the auditor reevaluating established materiality levels.

Choice "1" is incorrect. If the materiality level was established initially based on preliminary financial statement amounts and those amounts differ significantly from actual amounts, then this would be a circumstance that would require the auditor to reevaluate the established materiality levels.

Choice "2" is incorrect. A situation that would require reevaluation of established materiality levels include changes in circumstance, such as a major disposition of the entity's business.

Choice "4" is incorrect. A circumstance that would require reevaluation of established materiality levels include significant new contractual arrangements that draw attention to a particular aspect of a client's business that is separately disclosed in the financial statements.

Topic H

QUESTION 1

Choice "4" is correct.

Analytical procedures do not ordinarily provide information about the internal auditor.

Choices "1", "2", and "3" are incorrect. Discussions with management personnel, reviews of the internal auditor's work, and previous experience could all provide information relevant to the evaluation of competence and objectivity.

QUESTION 2

Choice "2" is correct.

An auditor may not divide responsibility with an auditor's specialist. If the auditor decides to express a modified opinion as a result of the work performed by the specialist, then the auditor may refer to the specialist and should indicate that the reference to the specialist does not reduce the auditor's responsibility for the audit opinion.

Choice "1" is incorrect. When an auditor decides to use the work of an auditor's specialist as audit evidence, the auditor should evaluate the competence, capabilities, and objectivity of the specialist. Evaluation of this may be acquired by obtaining knowledge of the specialist's qualifications.

Choice "3" is incorrect. When an auditor decides to use the work of an auditor's specialist as audit evidence, the auditor should evaluate the competence, capabilities, and objectivity of the specialist. Evaluation of this may be acquired by inquiring of the entity and the auditor's specialist about any known interests that the entity has with the auditor's external specialist that may affect that specialist's objectivity.

Choice "4" is incorrect. The external auditor should verify the adequacy of the work of the auditor's specialist. This may include reviewing the working papers of the auditor's specialist.

Auditing II

Topic I

Choice "3" is correct.

Reviewing confirmations of loans receivable and payable is useful for determining the existence of related party transactions because guarantees are commonly provided by or for related parties.

Choice "1" is incorrect because detection of unreported contingent liabilities is not a procedure that would assist the auditor in identifying related party transactions.

Choice "2" is incorrect because recurring transactions after year-end are a usual business occurrence. Related party transactions would most likely be nonrecurring.

Choice "4" is incorrect because while financial difficulties may be associated with related party transactions, it is unlikely that analytical procedures would assist the auditor in identifying such transactions.

Choice "4" is correct.

An illegal payment to a foreign official would most likely raise a question concerning possible noncompliance with laws and regulations.

Choice "1" is incorrect. Failure to retire a piece of obsolete equipment is not likely to raise a question about noncompliance with laws and regulations.

Choice "2" is incorrect. Failure to correct material internal control weaknesses may represent a conscious decision by management to accept the degree of risk because of cost or other considerations.

Choice "3" is incorrect. Receipt of governmental financial assistance most likely would not cause the auditor to raise a question about possible noncompliance with laws and regulations.

Topic J

Choice "3" is correct.

The auditor's overall responsibility is to obtain sufficient competent audit evidence to provide reasonable assurance that fair value measurements and disclosures are in conformity with GAAP.

Choice "1" is incorrect because while it is true that the auditor should determine whether management has the intent and ability to carry out courses of action that may affect fair values, this is just one part of evaluating fair value measurements and not the best description of the auditor's overall responsibility.

Choice "2" is incorrect because while it is true that the auditor should assess the risk of material misstatement of fair value measurements, this is done to determine the nature, timing, and extent of audit procedures. It is not the best representation of the auditor's overall responsibility.

Choice "4" is incorrect because *management* (and not the auditor) should make fair value measurements and disclosures in accordance with GAAP and should identify and support any significant assumptions used.

QUESTION 2

MCQ-09065

Choice "2" is correct.

The auditor should verify that all material estimates required by GAAP have been developed.

Choice "1" is incorrect. The auditor is responsible for auditing estimated amounts included in the financial statements, to determine that they are reasonable and properly presented and disclosed.

Choice "3" is incorrect. The auditor should focus on assumptions that are *subjective* (not objective), *sensitive* (not insensitive) to variation, and *deviate* from historical patterns, as these types of assumptions are more likely to result in unreasonable estimates.

Choice "4" is incorrect. Management (and not the auditor) bears responsibility for making reasonable estimates and including them in the financial statements.

Topic A

QUESTION 1

Choice "4" is correct.

A misstatement may not be an isolated occurrence. Identification of a misstatement that resulted from an inappropriate valuation method that has been widely applied by the entity may indicate that additional misstatements exist.

Choice "1" is incorrect. Management's enforcement of integrity and ethical values implies a stronger control environment, which may result in fewer misstatements, especially due to fraud.

Choice "2" is incorrect. The inclusion of several large, outstanding checks in the monthly bank reconciliation may be a normal occurrence and is not necessarily indicative of material misstatement.

Choice "3" is incorrect. Sometimes companies will outsource the internal audit function to another CPA firm. The CPA firm hired will perform the internal audit procedures and then report the results to management. Evidence of an internal audit function (outsourced or not) typically results in a reduction of misstatements.

Topic B

QUESTION 1

Choice "4" is correct.

By using statistical sampling, the auditor can quantify sampling risk to assist in limiting it to a level considered acceptable.

Choice "1" is incorrect because statistical sampling does not provide any advantage with respect to converting the test into a dual-purpose test.

Choice "2" is incorrect because statistical sampling still requires judgment to determine sample sizes. The tolerable rate of deviation, the likely rate of deviation, and the allowable risk of assessing control risk too low are all determined by the auditor's professional judgment.

Choice "3" is incorrect because statistical sampling does not afford greater assurance than a nonstatistical sample of the same size. It only provides the auditor with a better measure of the sufficiency of the evidence found, and helps to evaluate the results found.

QUESTION 2

Choice "2" is correct.

Attribute sampling is primarily used to test controls, such as proper approval of purchase orders.

Choice "1" is incorrect. Variables sampling is typically used in substantive testing, such as confirming accounts receivable balances.

Choice "3" is incorrect. Variables sampling is typically used in substantive testing, such as verifying proper extensions and footings of invoices.

Choice "4" is incorrect. Variables sampling is typically used in substantive testing, such as testing that cash receipts are appropriately credited to customer accounts.

Auditing III

QUESTION 3

Choice "1" is correct.

The risk of incorrect rejection and the risk of assessing control risk too high relate to the efficiency of the audit. These two errors generally result in an auditor performing unnecessary additional procedures.

Choice "2" is incorrect because the application of additional procedures will ordinarily still lead the auditor to the appropriate conclusion.

Choice "3" is incorrect because these risks do not relate directly to selection of the items included in the sample.

Choice "4" is incorrect because these risks do not relate directly to quality controls.

QUESTION 4

Choice "4" is correct.

All else being equal, the sample size required to achieve the auditor's objective increases as the auditor's assessment of tolerable misstatement for the balance or class decreases.

Choice "1" is incorrect because a greater reliance on internal control will lead to a smaller sample size in a substantive test of details.

Choice "2" is incorrect because greater reliance upon analytical procedures will reduce the need for reliance on substantive tests of details, which in turn will result in a smaller sample size.

Choice "3" is incorrect because as fewer errors are expected, a smaller sample size would be used.

QUESTION 5

Choice "4" is correct.

The auditor will reduce reliance on a control if the upper deviation rate exceeds the tolerable rate. The upper deviation rate consists of the sample deviation rate plus an allowance for sampling risk. Therefore, if the sample deviation rate plus the allowance for sampling risk exceeds the tolerable rate, that is equivalent to the upper deviation rate exceeding the tolerable rate.

Choice "1" is incorrect because if the sample deviation rate plus the allowance for sampling risk equals the tolerable rate, the auditor may still place the planned amount of reliance on the control.

Choice "2" is incorrect because whether the actual sample deviation rate is less than the expected deviation rate is irrelevant for making decisions about planned reliance levels.

Choice "3" is incorrect because if the tolerable rate less the allowance for sampling risk exceeds the sample rate of deviation, then the upper deviation rate is less than the tolerable rate. This situation supports the planned reliance, and no reduction in planned reliance would be necessary.

Topic C

QUESTION 1

Choice "3" is correct.

Confirmation of accounts receivable is a substantive test, not a test of controls.

Choice "1" is incorrect. Records documenting the usage of computer programs may indicate whether access is appropriately controlled.

Choice "2" is incorrect. Examination of canceled supporting documents helps the auditor determine whether this control is being appropriately applied.

Choice "4" is incorrect. Signatures on authorization forms help the auditor determine whether or not required authorizations are received.

Topic D

QUESTION 1

Choice "2" is correct.

Interest costs related to construction of a fixed asset by a company may be capitalized to the asset being constructed. This bests explains the reason for the increase in debt outstanding (acquisition of new debt) and interest expense staying approximately the same (the additional interest expense from the construction loan is being capitalized to the construction of the building).

Choice "1" is incorrect. If the company paid off a significant portion of debt, then the overall debt outstanding probably would decrease, not increase.

Choice "3" is incorrect. The company only invests in debt that has a fixed interest rate; therefore, a decrease in the Federal Reserve rate probably would not affect their interest expense.

Choice "4" is incorrect. Acquiring a new loan at midyear would increase the debt outstanding, but would not explain why interest expense stayed approximately the same.

QUESTION 2

Choice "4" is correct.

Accounts receivable turnover is calculated as net sales divided by average receivables. Allowing a grace period for customer payments is likely to increase the average receivable balance, thus decreasing accounts receivable turnover.

Choice "1" is incorrect. Accounts receivable turnover is calculated as net sales divided by average receivables. Early payment incentives are likely to reduce average receivables, thus increasing accounts receivable turnover.

Choice "2" is incorrect. Accounts receivable turnover is calculated as net sales divided by average receivables. If credit policy is tightened, there are less likely to be delinquent customers and the average receivable balance should decline, thus increasing accounts receivable turnover.

Choice "3" is incorrect. Accounts receivable turnover is calculated as net sales divided by average receivables. Implementation of more aggressive collection policies will tend to result in a decrease in average receivables, thus increasing accounts receivable turnover.

Auditing III

Topic E

QUESTION 1   MCQ-08112

Choice "3" is correct.

Expenses for the current year are not complete if an expense occurring in one year is not recorded until the following year.

Choice "1" is incorrect. Accuracy relates to recording at an appropriate amount.

Choice "2" is incorrect. Classification relates to recording in the proper accounts.

Choice "4" is incorrect. Occurrence relates to recording only events that have occurred during the given year.

QUESTION 2   MCQ-09839

Choice "4" is correct.

Examining open vouchers as part of the search for *unrecorded liabilities* is a substantive procedure.

Choice "1" is incorrect. Verifying that the vouchers payable package is properly approved is a test of controls, not a substantive procedure.

Choice "2" is incorrect. Observation of the payroll distribution on an unannounced basis is a test of controls, which involves verifying that all personnel being paid are actually employed by the company.

Choice "3" is incorrect. Observing the preparation of the accounts receivable aging schedule is a test of controls, not a substantive procedure.

Topic F

QUESTION 1   MCQ-09833

Choice "3" is correct.

An acceptable alternative procedure is to examine the applicable sales order, shipping document, and subsequent cash receipts.

Choice "1" is incorrect. Generally, an auditor would not visit the client's customer and review documents in their possession. An appropriate alternative procedure is to review the specific subsequent cash receipts, shipping documentation, and invoice to verify the existence of the receivable.

Choice "2" is incorrect. Obtaining an aging of accounts receivable and tracing it to the general ledger control account would provide evidence about the completeness, not existence, assertion.

Choice "4" is incorrect. Examining subsequent cash disbursements and related receiving reports would be an appropriate alternative procedure when testing accounts payable for completeness when the accounts payable confirmations are not received.

Auditing III

QUESTION 2

Choice "2" is correct.

Lapping best describes the employee fraud scheme. Lapping occurs when current receipts of cash are withheld and not recorded. Subsequent receipts are applied to prior accounts.

Choice "1" is incorrect. This scheme does not describe kiting. Kiting occurs when a check drawn on one bank is deposited in another bank and no record is made of the disbursement.

Choice "3" is incorrect. This scheme most likely is not identity theft. Identity theft occurs when someone uses a person's personal information for financial gain (e.g., makes purchases).

Choice "4" is incorrect. Fraudulent financial reporting involves intentional misstatements or omissions of amounts designed to deceive financial statement users. It does not appear that the employee is trying to deceive financial statement users. Lapping is more likely to be categorized as a misappropriation of assets, which involves theft of an entity's financial assets.

Topic G

QUESTION 1

Choice "1" is correct.

The daily sales summary will include all "billed" sales for a particular day. Comparing this summary to the postings to the accounts receivable ledger will provide evidence regarding whether billed sales are correctly posted.

Choice "2" is incorrect. Comparing sales invoices to shipping documents provides evidence that invoiced sales have been shipped.

Choice "3" is incorrect. Reconciling the accounts receivable ledger to the control account will not provide assurance that all billed sales were posted. The receivable ledger and the control account may both have omitted the sales.

Choice "4" is incorrect. Comparing shipments with sales invoices provides evidence regarding whether all shipments have been invoiced, not whether billed sales are correctly posted to accounts receivable.

QUESTION 2

Choice "2" is correct.

Tracing shipments to sales invoices would provide evidence that shipments to customers were properly invoiced.

Choice "1" is incorrect. Tracing from invoices to shipping documents would provide evidence that sales billed to customers were actually shipped.

Choice "3" is incorrect. Tracing from invoices to shipping documents would provide evidence that shipments to customers were invoiced, but does not necessarily indicate that invoices were recorded as sales.

Choice "4" is incorrect. The auditor would compare the signed purchase order to shipping documents to determine if all goods ordered by the customer were shipped.

Auditing III

QUESTION 3

MCQ-09849

Choice "4" is correct.

An auditor most likely would compare subsequent bank statements (specifically looking for cash payments made after the balance sheet date) with the accounts payable listing in searching for unrecorded payables. The auditor is looking for payables that should have been recorded as of the balance sheet date, but were not.

Choice "1" is incorrect. Obtaining a sample of vendor statements and recalculating the invoice amount would provide evidence about the accuracy of the invoice amount.

Choice "2" is incorrect. Obtaining the accounts payable listing and agreeing to subsequent cash payments provides evidence about existence, not completeness.

Choice "3" is incorrect. Comparing cash disbursements made before year-end with vendor invoices would not help the auditor search for unrecorded payables. Cash payments made before year-end for vendor invoices should result in the payable being eliminated.

QUESTION 4

MCQ-08325

Choice "4" is correct.

Companies sometimes erroneously expense property and equipment acquisitions rather than capitalizing them as assets. An analysis of repair and maintenance accounts may reveal such errors.

Choice "1" is incorrect because while auditors will want to determine that noncapitalizable expenses for repairs and maintenance have been recorded in the proper period, analyzing only the recorded entries is an incomplete test. The auditor would also need to look at payments that were not recorded in the current period, in case they should have been.

Choice "2" is incorrect because expenditures for property and equipment would not be included in repair and maintenance accounts.

Choice "3" is incorrect because analyzing items already included in the repair and maintenance account would not identify noncapitalizable expenditures that have been erroneously capitalized.

QUESTION 5

MCQ-08124

Choice "1" is correct.

Payroll is generally determined in a fairly objective manner and is easily tested by the auditor. As such, specific representations with respect to payroll are not often requested.

Choice "2" is incorrect. Segregation of duties is a key control within the payroll cycle. The auditor should verify that the functions of authorization, record keeping, and custody are appropriately segregated.

Choice "3" is incorrect. Year-end payroll accruals are fairly easy to recalculate, and such recalculation provides good audit evidence supporting financial statement amounts.

Choice "4" is incorrect. Payroll is fairly predictable and thus is often compared with standards and budgets.

QUESTION 6

Choice "3" is correct.

The legality of a dividend depends in part on whether it has been properly authorized. Thus, the auditor must determine that proper authorization exists, as both cash and stock dividends affect retained earnings.

Choice "1" is incorrect because only a memo entry is required for a stock split.

Choice "2" is incorrect because the write-down of an account receivable will not, in general, be recorded in retained earnings.

Choice "4" is incorrect because gains from the disposition of treasury shares are recorded in paid-in capital accounts.

Topic H

QUESTION 1

Choice "3" is correct.

During a tour of the manufacturing plant or production facility, the auditor should be alert for items that appear to be old, obsolete, or defective.

Choice "1" is incorrect. Testing the mathematical accuracy of the inventory report would determine that the numerical amounts are computed correctly, but would not provide evidence about whether the inventory is slow-moving, defective, or obsolete after manufacture.

Choice "2" is incorrect. Inquiry of management about pledged or assigned inventory would provide evidence about the rights and obligation of the inventory, but would not inform the auditor about slow-moving, defective, or obsolete inventory.

Choice "4" is incorrect. Testing the computation of standard overhead rates relates to the accumulation of costs during the manufacturing process, and not to whether the inventory is slow-moving, defective, or obsolete after manufacture.

QUESTION 2

Choice "1" is correct.

A custodial statement provides valid and relevant external evidence regarding the existence of securities.

Choice "2" is incorrect. The client's securities ledger is internal evidence, and as such it is not as valid as a custodial statement.

Choice "3" is incorrect. Broker's advices regarding purchases and sales provide valid external evidence about transactions occurring during the year, but a custodial statement provides more direct evidence about the existence of securities as of the year-end date.

Choice "4" is incorrect. A year-end listing of market prices is not relevant to the existence of marketable securities, although it would provide evidence about the valuation of such securities.

Auditing III

Topic I

QUESTION 1

Choice "2" is correct.

The attorney's refusal to respond when the attorney has given substantial attention to the matter would represent a scope limitation. Depending on materiality, this may result in a qualified opinion or disclaimer of opinion.

Choice "1" is incorrect. A refusal to permit inquiry will generally result in a disclaimer of opinion or withdrawal from the audit.

Choice "3" is incorrect. If the auditor is satisfied that financial statement disclosure is adequate, no modification to the opinion would be required.

Choice "4" is incorrect. Lawyers may limit their replies to matters to which they have given substantial attention.

QUESTION 2

Choice "3" is correct.

The primary purpose of an external inquiry of the client's attorney is to obtain corroboration of information provided by management regarding litigation, claims, and assessments.

Choices "1" and "2" are incorrect. The auditor's external inquiry of the client's attorney provides information about litigation, claims, and assessments, such as the nature of the matter, the progress of the case, the degree of likelihood of an unfavorable outcome, and an estimate of potential loss. It does not provide information about the client's controls with respect to recognizing the financial statement impact of such matters.

Choice "4" is incorrect. The client's attorney provides information such as the nature of the matter, the progress of the case, the degree of likelihood of an unfavorable outcome, and an estimate of potential loss, but does not comment or provide advice regarding the fair presentation of such matters in the financial statements.

Topic J

QUESTION 1

Choice "3" is correct.

Calibro should issue an unmodified opinion with an emphasis-of-matter paragraph describing the situation.

Choice "1" is incorrect. In situations where there is substantial doubt about the entity's ability to continue as a going concern, the auditor generally should add an emphasis-of-matter paragraph (not other-matter paragraph) to the unmodified opinion.

Choice "2" is incorrect. In situations where there is substantial doubt about the entity's ability to continue as a going concern, the auditor generally should add an emphasis-of-matter paragraph to the unmodified opinion. There is no need to qualify the opinion.

Choice "4" is incorrect. In situations where there is substantial doubt about the entity's ability to continue as a going concern, the auditor generally should add an emphasis-of-matter paragraph to the unmodified opinion. As long as the auditor adds the appropriate explanatory language, there would be no need to withdraw from the engagement.

QUESTION 2

Choice "4" is correct.

Management's ability to negotiate reductions of required dividends will decrease required cash outflows, and thereby increase the likelihood that the entity will be able to continue as a going concern.

Choices "1", "2", and "3" are incorrect because they involve spending cash, rather than reducing outflows of cash.

Topic K

QUESTION 1

Choice "3" is correct.

Significant deficiencies in the design or operation of internal control are control weaknesses that are important enough to merit attention by those charged with governance.

Choice "1" is incorrect because information that significantly contradicts the auditor's going concern assumption is not considered a significant deficiency.

Choice "2" is incorrect because fraud perpetrated by high-level managers should be reported to the audit committee (i.e. those charged with governance). However, it does not necessarily represent a significant deficiency in internal control.

Choice "4" is incorrect because fraud should be reported to an appropriate level of management, and sometimes to the audit committee (i.e. those charged with governance). However, it does not necessarily represent a significant deficiency in internal control.

Topic L

QUESTION 1

Choice "2" is correct.

U.S. GAAS require the date of the written representations to be the date of the auditor's report.

Choice "1" is incorrect. According to ISAs, not U.S. GAAS, the management representation letter should be dated as near as possible to, but not after, the date of the auditor's report.

Choice "3" is incorrect. U.S. GAAS require the date of the written representations to be the date of the auditor's report. The auditor will complete the audit after the date of the financial statements.

Choice "4" is incorrect. U.S. GAAS require the date of the written representations to be the date of the auditor's report. The auditor will complete the audit after the date of the financial statements.

Auditing III

Topic M

MCQ-08118

Choice "3" is correct.

The acquisition provided evidence of a condition which came into existence after year-end [a "Type 2" (nonrecognized) subsequent event] and therefore the proper accounting approach would be note disclosure rather than adjustment.

Choice "1" is incorrect because adjustments are only appropriate for subsequent events which provide evidence that the condition was in existence at year-end ["Type 1" (recognized) events].

Choice "2" is incorrect because the auditor does not issue financial statements for the client.

Choice "4" is incorrect because the opinion paragraph of the report need not be modified. The auditor might choose to add an explanatory paragraph emphasizing the matter, but is not required to do so.

MCQ-09050

Choice "3" is correct.

The auditor has an active responsibility to investigate subsequent events between the date of the financial statements and the date of the auditor's report, and must also consider the effect of any events occurring after the date of the auditor's report that come to his/her attention.

Choice "1" is incorrect. The auditor has no active responsibility to investigate events occurring after the date of the auditor's report, unless such events come to his or her attention.

Choice "2" is incorrect. The auditor has an active responsibility to investigate the 2/1/Year 2 event, but also may have some level of responsibility with respect to the 3/1/Year 2 event. Despite the fact that it occurred after the date of the auditor's report, if the event comes to the auditor's attention, it cannot be ignored.

Choice "4" is incorrect. The auditor has an active responsibility to investigate subsequent events between the date of the financial statements and the date of the auditor's report, and must also consider the effect of any events occurring after the date of the auditor's report that come to his/her attention.

Topic N

QUESTION 1

Choice "4" is correct.

The question addresses subsequent discovery of facts that may have existed at the balance sheet date that the auditor should have known about during the audit. Discovery of information related to a material *unrecorded* expense that occurred during the year under audit most likely would result in the auditor making further inquiries about the previously issued financial statements.

Choice "1" is incorrect. The issuance of a bond for a material amount is an example of a subsequent event occurring after the date of the auditor's report that the auditor has no obligation to investigate. The issuance of the bond does not provide additional information about the previously issued financial statements, nor did the issuance exist at the date of the audit report.

Choice "2" is incorrect. The loss of a plant is an example of a subsequent event occurring after the date of the auditor's report that the auditor has no obligation to investigate. The loss of the plant does not provide additional information about the previously issued financial statements, nor did the loss of the plant exist at the date of the audit report.

Choice "3" is incorrect. The purchase of a business is an example of a subsequent event occurring after the date of the auditor's report that the auditor has no obligation to investigate. The purchase of the business does not provide additional information about the previously issued financial statements audit. In addition, the purchase of the business occurred after the date of the auditor's report.

Auditing Final Review

Topic A

QUESTION 1

MCQ-09769

Choice "4" is correct.

Determining the type of work to be performed on the components is not required when the group auditor decides to make reference to the component auditor. The group auditor should determine the type of work to be performed on the financial information of the components when assuming responsibility for the work of the component auditor.

Choice "1" is incorrect. The group auditor should be satisfied with the independence of the component auditor even when the group auditor references the component auditor in the report.

Choice "2" is incorrect. One of the requirements to reference the component auditor in the group auditor's report is that the component auditor's report is not restricted.

Choice "3" is incorrect. The group auditor should be satisfied with the competence of the component auditor even when the group auditor references the component auditor in the report.

QUESTION 2

MCQ-09768

Choice "3" is correct.

Financial statements that are prepared in accordance with a special purpose framework require the use of an emphasis-of-matter paragraph in the auditor's report.

Choice "1" is incorrect. An other-matter paragraph is required when there is an alert in the audit report that restricts the use of the audit report.

Choice "2" is incorrect. An other-matter paragraph is required when prior to the audit report date, the auditor identifies a material inconsistency in other information that is included in the document containing audited financial statements that management refuses to revise.

Choice "4" is incorrect. An other-matter paragraph is required when the auditor chooses to report on supplementary information presented with the financial statements in the auditor's report, rather than in a separate report.

QUESTION 3

MCQ-09764

Choice "4" is correct.

Inadequate disclosure of a material item or event results in a qualified or adverse opinion.

Choice "1" is incorrect. Although the general rule in adequately disclosed going concern cases is to add an emphasis-of-matter paragraph to an unmodified opinion, the auditor is not prohibited from choosing to disclaim an opinion due to a going concern uncertainty

Choice "2" is incorrect. Management's refusal to permit inquiry of the attorneys generally will result in a disclaimer of opinion or withdrawal from the audit.

Choice "3" is incorrect. When the auditor is not independent but is required by law or regulation to report on the financial statements, the auditor should disclaim an opinion and should specifically state that the auditor is not independent.

Auditing IV

QUESTION 4

MCQ-09041

Choice "2" is correct.

Randall may revise the prior opinion, but must include an emphasis-of-matter or other-matter paragraph describing the situation and including the date and type of the previous opinion, the reason for the previous opinion, the changes that have occurred, and a statement that the new opinion differs from the old.

Choice "1" is incorrect. Randall may revise the prior opinion if the situation warrants such revision.

Choice "3" is incorrect. Randall may revise the prior opinion if the situation warrants such revision, and is not prohibited from issuing a report on the comparative financial statements.

Choice "4" is incorrect. Randall may revise the prior opinion, but must include an emphasis-of-matter or other-matter paragraph describing the situation and including the date and type of the previous opinion, the reason for the previous opinion, the changes that have occurred, and a statement that the new opinion differs from the old.

Topic B

QUESTION 1

MCQ-09864

Choice "2" is correct.

Entity-level controls are high-level controls that have a pervasive effect on the company's internal control. Entity-level controls include controls related to the period-end financial reporting process, such as management's procedures used to initiate, authorize, and record journal entries into the general ledger.

Choice "1" is incorrect. An entity-level control exists at the client and is independent of the audit. Therefore, the auditor's adherence to a system of quality control would not be considered an entity-level control.

Choice "3" is incorrect. Entity-level controls are high-level controls that have a pervasive effect on the company's internal control. Examples of entity-level controls include controls related to control environment, monitoring the results of operations, centralized processing, period-end financial reporting process and the company's risk assessment process. Preparation of an aging schedule relates to the revenue cycle and is a control at the assertion level.

Choice "4" is incorrect. Entity-level controls are high-level controls that that have a pervasive effect on the company's internal control. Creating a duplicate listing of checks after receipt of a customer check by mail is a control related to the revenue cycle and is a control at the assertion level.

Topic C

QUESTION 1

MCQ-09064

Choice "1" is correct.

The auditor of a nonissuer may be engaged to express an opinion on the design and/or operating effectiveness of the entity's internal control. This is considered an audit engagement. Note that an audit of internal control should be integrated with an audit of the financial statements.

Choice "2" is incorrect. The auditor of a nonissuer may not express an opinion as a result of a financial statement audit, but may report on significant deficiencies or material weaknesses noted during the audit. The report on control deficiencies noted should specifically state that the auditor is not expressing an opinion on the effectiveness of internal control.

Choice "3" is incorrect. A financial statement audit includes consideration of internal control as a basis for designing audit procedures, not as a basis for expressing an opinion. An auditor of a nonissuer may report on significant deficiencies or material weaknesses noted during the audit, but is prohibited from expressing an opinion based solely on the audit.

Choice "4" is incorrect. While an auditor of a nonissuer is required to communicate significant deficiencies or material weaknesses to management and those charged with governance, this type of report does not provide an opinion on the operating effectiveness of the entity's internal control.

QUESTION 2

MCQ-09861

Choice "3" is correct.

A material weakness in internal control, which is a control deficiency, or a combination of control deficiencies in internal control such that there is a reasonable possibility that a material misstatement of the entity's financial statements will not be prevented, or detected and corrected on a timely basis, requires the auditor to issue an adverse opinion.

Choice "1" is incorrect. A material weakness would result in an adverse, not unmodified, opinion.

Choice "2" is incorrect. A material weakness would result in an adverse, not qualified, opinion.

Choice "4" is incorrect. A disclaimer of opinion is rendered when there is a scope limitation.

Auditing IV

Topic D

QUESTION 1

Choice "2" is correct.

An engagement for agreed-upon procedures provides no assurance, which means that a disclaimer of opinion is rendered on the subject matter. Specifically, the report should state that "We do not express an opinion," which is a disclaimer of opinion.

Choice "1" is incorrect. The procedures do not need to be comparable to those performed in a compilation. The procedures that the practitioner and specified parties agree upon may be as limited or as extensive as the specified parties desire.

Choice "3" is incorrect. The report includes a listing of procedures performed and the related findings, but does not provide any assurance on these items.

Choice "4" is incorrect. The sufficiency of procedures is solely the responsibility of the specified parties, not the practitioner.

QUESTION 2

Choice "4" is correct.

Financial forecasts are considered prospective financial statements, and they are appropriate for general use.

Choice "1" is incorrect because financial projections are only appropriate for the party responsible for preparing them or for third parties with whom the responsible party is negotiating directly.

Choices "2" and "3" are incorrect because partial presentations and pro forma financial statements are not considered prospective financial statements.

Topic E

QUESTION 1

Choice "3" is correct.

Statements on Standards for Accounting and Review Services do not apply to preparing a working trial balance or to preparing standard monthly journal entries. Accordingly, no compilation or review report needs to be issued when these services are provided.

Choices "1", "2", and "4" are incorrect, based on the above explanation.

Auditing IV

QUESTION 2

Choice "1" is correct.

Before issuing a compilation report, an accountant should read the compiled financial statements and consider whether they are appropriate in form and free from obvious material errors.

Choice "2" is incorrect. Inquiry and analytical review procedures are performed as part of a review engagement, not as part of a compilation engagement.

Choice "3" is incorrect. A representation letter is obtained in audit and review engagements, but is not required for compilation engagements.

Choice "4" is incorrect. Accounts receivable confirmations would be sent during an audit, but not during a compilation engagement.

QUESTION 3

Choice "3" is correct.

A change in client requirements represents an acceptable reason for a change in engagement.

Choice "1" is incorrect. Generally, refusal to provide a signed representation letter is considered an unacceptable reason for the change. In addition, the auditor would not be able to issue a review report without a representation letter.

Choice "2" is incorrect. The client's refusal to allow correspondence with legal counsel is not an acceptable reason for the change.

Choice "4" is incorrect. The client's attempt to create deceptive financial statements is not an acceptable reason for the change.

QUESTION 4

Choice "2" is correct.

The predecessor accountant is not required to obtain a letter of representation from management before reissuing a compilation report. This procedure is required when an audit, not compilation, report is reissued.

Choice "1" is incorrect. The predecessor accountant is required to read the financial statements and the report of the current period before reissuing a compilation report.

Choice "3" is incorrect. The predecessor accountant is required to compare the prior period financial statements with those issued previously and currently before reissuing a compilation report.

Choice "4" is incorrect. The predecessor accountant is required to obtain a letter from the successor accountants before reissuing a compilation report.

Auditing IV

QUESTION 5

Choice "3" is correct.

When issuing letters for underwriters, an accountant typically provides positive assurance concerning the compliance of the audited financial statements with the requirements of the SEC Act.

Choice "1" is incorrect. The auditor may provide negative, not positive assurance, for financial statements that have been reviewed.

Choice "2" is incorrect. In a comfort letter, no comment should be made regarding the compliance of MD&A with SEC rules and regulations.

Choice "4" is incorrect. The auditor should not comment or provide any assurance on qualitative disclosures and market-sensitive instruments in a comfort letter.

Topic F

QUESTION 1

Choice "3" is correct.

A review report states that a review includes primarily applying analytical procedures to management's financial data and making inquiries of company management.

Choice "1" is incorrect because the review report does not state that limited assurance is provided. The report simply states that the accountant is not aware of any material modifications that should be made to the financial statement.

Choice "2" is incorrect because an audit report, not a review report, refers to "examining on a test basis." A compilation report, not a review report, refers to "information that is the representation of management."

Choice "4" is incorrect because although a review does not contemplate obtaining corroborating evidential matter or applying certain other procedures ordinarily performed during an audit, this is not stated in the report. The review report simply states that a review is substantially less in scope than an audit.

Topic G

QUESTION 1

Choice "4" is correct.

The auditor should read the letter to the shareholders (considered other information) and verify the information is materially consistent with the information presented in the audited financial statements.

Choice "1" is incorrect. The audited financial statements may be contained in a document that contains additional financial information that is outside the audited financial statements. In addition, the auditor's opinion is on the basic financial statements, not the entire document that the financial statements may accompany.

Choice "2" is incorrect. The auditor is not required to reference the other information in the audit report. However, the auditor *may* choose to include an other-matter paragraph disclaiming an opinion on the other information.

Choice "3" is incorrect. The auditor should inquire of management regarding the purpose of the supplementary information and the criteria used to prepare the information when engaged to report on the supplementary information. The auditor is not engaged to examine this information, so the auditor is not required to perform those inquiries.

QUESTION 2

Choice "4" is correct.

With respect to the supplementary information, Jorge should perform limited procedures in order to determine whether required supplementary information is included and is presented in conformity with GAAP requirements.

Choice "1" is incorrect. Jorge may accept this engagement, but must perform limited procedures in order to determine whether required supplementary information is included and is presented in conformity with GAAP requirements.

Choice "2" is incorrect. Jorge must perform limited procedures in order to determine whether required supplementary information is included and is presented in conformity with GAAP requirements.

Choice "3" is incorrect. Jorge may accept this engagement and should perform limited procedures with respect to the required supplementary information. There is no requirement that an attest engagement be performed.

QUESTION 3

Choice "3" is correct.

The appropriate form of audit report is dependent upon the expected distribution of the financial statements. If distribution is to occur outside the United States only, the auditor may use either the other country's audit report, the report set out in the ISAs, or a U.S. form with reference to the other country's standards. If there is to be distribution within the U.S., a U.S. form report with an emphasis-of-matter paragraph is required.

Choice "1" is incorrect. The other country's auditing standards do not determine the appropriate form of audit report for financial statements prepared in accordance with a financial reporting framework generally accepted in another country.

Choice "2" is incorrect. The geographic location of the company does not determine the appropriate form of audit report for financial statements prepared in accordance with a financial reporting framework generally accepted in another country.

Choice "4" is incorrect. Countries generally do not have reciprocity agreements with respect to the appropriate form of audit report.

Topic H

QUESTION 1

Choice "2" is correct.

Audits performed in accordance with government auditing standards require a written communication regarding the auditor's work on internal control. Generally accepted auditing standards only require written communication about internal control when significant deficiencies are noted.

Choice "1" is incorrect. Both GAAS and GAGAS require an opinion on the financial statements taken as a whole.

Choice "3" is incorrect. Neither GAAS nor GAGAS audits require an opinion on internal control over financial reporting.

Choice "4" is incorrect. An opinion on the financial statements taken as a whole *is* required by both GAAS and GAGAS.

Auditing IV

Choice "4" is correct.

The provisions of the Single Audit Act apply to entities that receive and expend federal financial awards equal to or in excess of $750,000.

Choice "1" is incorrect. Pure receipt of federal financial assistance does not mandate application of the provisions of the Single Audit Act to an entity's financial statements. Federal financial assistance must be expended by an entity in an amount equal to or in excess of $750,000 to result in an audit subject to 2 CFR 200 single audit requirements.

Choice "2" is incorrect. Pure receipt of federal financial assistance does not mandate application of the provisions of the Single Audit Act to an entity's financial statements. Federal financial assistance must be expended by an entity in an amount equal to or in excess of $750,000 to result in an audit subject to 2 CFR 200 single audit requirements.

Choice "3" is incorrect. The provisions of the Single Audit Act apply to entities that receive and expend federal financial awards equal to or in excess of $750,000.

Choice "2" is correct.

The requirement is to determine the proper scope of a government audit. The Government Accountability Office's Yellow Book suggests that in addition to financial statements, such an audit may include consideration of (1) program results; (2) compliance with laws and regulations; and (3) economy and efficiency.

Choice "1" is incorrect because government audits may involve expression of an opinion on economy and efficiency.

Choice "3" is incorrect because government audits may involve expression of an opinion on program results.

Choice "4" is incorrect because government audits may involve expression of an opinion on compliance.

Topic I

Choice "2" is correct.

An auditor's report should include a restricted use paragraph and an alert to readers about the preparation of the financial statements in accordance with a special purpose framework when the financial statements are prepared on the contractual basis of accounting.

Choice "1" is incorrect. An auditor's report should include an alert to readers about the preparation of the financial statements in accordance with a special purpose framework when the financial statements are prepared on the cash basis of accounting. There is no requirement that the auditor's report must be restricted for this type of framework.

Choice "3" is incorrect. Financial statements prepared using IFRS do not require a restricted use paragraph in the auditor's report. In addition, IFRS is not considered a special purpose framework.

Choice "4" is incorrect. An auditor's report should include an alert to readers about the preparation of the financial statements in accordance with a special purpose framework when the financial statements are prepared on the tax basis of accounting. There is no requirement that the auditor's report must be restricted for this type of framework.

QUESTION 2   MCQ-09785

Choice "2" is correct.

The auditor modified the opinion on the complete financial statements due to a material misstatement of inventory and cost of goods sold. Because the modification is relevant to the audit opinion on inventory, the auditor should express an adverse opinion on inventory.

Choice "1" is incorrect. Qualified opinions are not permitted on an audit of a specific element when the modification of the opinion on the complete financial statements was due to the specific element.

Choice "3" is incorrect. The auditor would render a disclaimer of opinion on inventory if the opinion on the complete financial statements were modified due to a scope limitation related to inventory.

Choice "4" is incorrect. The auditor may not issue an unmodified opinion on inventory because the auditor modified the opinion on the complete financial statements due to a material misstatement of inventory. Because the modification is relevant to the audit opinion on inventory, the auditor should express an adverse opinion on inventory.

QUESTION 3   MCQ-08119

Choice "3" is correct.

The report on a specific element of a financial statement follows the standard auditor's report very closely, referring to GAAS in the auditor's responsibility paragraph and GAAP in the opinion paragraph.

Choice "1" is incorrect because an audit of the complete financial statements is not required, although the audit of a specific element of the financial statements may be done in conjunction with an audit of the complete set of financial statements.

Choice "2" is incorrect because an unmodified opinion on a specific element may be expressed as long as 1) the opinion on the specific element is not published with and does not accompany the auditor's report on the complete set of financial statements and 2) the element does not encompass a major portion of the financial statements and is not, or is not based on, stockholder's equity or net income. Note that if the modified opinion on the complete set of financial statements is relevant to the audit of the specific element of the financial statements, then the auditor should:

■ Express an adverse opinion on the specific element when an adverse opinion is expressed on the complete set of financial statements

■ Express a disclaimer of opinion on the specific element when a disclaimer of opinion is expressed on the complete set of financial statements

Choice "4" is incorrect because a restrictive use paragraph is only required if the element was prepared to comply with a contract or agreement rather than in accordance with GAAP.

Auditing IV

QUESTION 4

Choice "2" is correct.

A report on a client's compliance with a contractual agreement, assuming the report is prepared in connection with a financial statement audit of the complete financial statements should include a restriction as to the use of the report.

Choice "1" is incorrect. A report on financial statements prepared on the tax basis of accounting does not require a restriction as to the use of the report.

Choice "3" is incorrect. Reports on a single financial statement do not require restriction as to the use of the report.

Choice "4" is incorrect. A report on the examination of a financial forecast does not require a restriction on the use of the report.